EQ+IQ=

BEST LEADERSHIP PRACTICES
for Caring and Successful Schools

We would like to dedicate this book to James Comer, whose inspiration, dedication, generosity, persistence, and unflagging belief in the potential of every youngster regardless of degree of risk or disadvantage continue to be catalysts and models for those in the field who care deeply about children.
He is the embodiment of EQ + IQ.

EQ+IQ=

BEST LEADERSHIP PRACTICES
for Caring and Successful Schools

edited by
Maurice J. Elias
Harriett Arnold
Cynthia Steiger Hussey

CORWIN PRESS, INC.
A Sage Publications Company
Thousand Oaks, California

For information:

Corwin Press, Inc.
A Sage Publications Company
2455 Teller Road
Thousand Oaks, California 91320
www.corwinpress.com

Sage Publications Ltd.
6 Bonhill Street
London EC2A 4PU
United Kingdom

Sage Publications India Pvt. Ltd.
B-42 Panchsheel Enclave
New Delhi 110 017 India

Printed in the United States of America

Library of Congress Cataloging-in-Publication Data

EQ + IQ = Best leadership practices for caring and successful schools /
edited by Maurice J. Elias, Harriett Arnold, and Cynthia Steiger Hussey.
    p. cm.
Includes bibliographical references and index.
ISBN 0-7619-4520-2 (cloth)
ISBN 0-7619-4521-0 (paper)
   1. Educational leadership-United States. 2. School improvement
programs-United States. 3. Emotional intelligence. I. Title: EQ and IQ.
II. Title: EQ plus IQ. III. Elias, Maurice J. IV. Arnold, Harriett. V.
Hussey, Cynthia Steiger.
LB2805 .E69 2003
371.2—dc21

                                        2002014620

This book is printed on acid-free paper.

02 03 04 05 10 9 8 7 6 5 4 3 2 1

Acquisitions Editor:	Faye Zucker
Editorial Assistant:	Julia Parnell
Copy Editor:	Elizabeth Budd
Production Editor:	Denise Santoyo
Typesetter:	C&M Digitals (P) Ltd
Indexer:	Molly Hall
Cover Designer:	Tracy E. Miller
Production Artist:	Michelle Lee

Contents

Preface

The events of September 11, 2001, have made the already-challenging mission of schools even more so, demanding that we prepare children for the tests of life and not merely a life of tests (Elias, 2001). School leaders must find ways for students to emerge from their education experiences knowledgeable, responsible, nonviolent, drug-free, and caring, as well as imbued with the social and emotional skills needed to deal with the opportunities and risks that life presents in abundance.

But even before September 11, there was growing recognition that the definition of what it means to be well educated must expand if students are to be prepared for adult roles in the 21st century. Daniel Goleman's book *Emotional Intelligence* (Goleman, 1995) was the lightning rod for this recognition—not only in the United States but in countries speaking the 30 languages into which the book was translated. "EQ," as emotional intelligence has come to be known, has a rightful place alongside IQ in conceptualizing what it means to be smart. In fact, extensive research since 1995 has shown that EQ is an essential part of success in academics, in the workplace, and in civic and family life. Like IQ, the role of EQ might best be described as necessary but not sufficient. IQ + EQ, however, seems to be an unbeatable combination.

Brain research supports the movement toward integration of IQ and EQ in education. Educators already realize this from the acceptance in schools of many of the tenets of multiple intelligences theory and practice. Emotional intelligence is strongly linked to Howard Gardner's interpersonal and intrapersonal intelligences, as well as to his emerging area of spiritual intelligence. The recent work of LeDoux and Damasio, Caine and Caine, Wolfe, Jensen, Sylwester, and others—striving to understand how instruction can be more "brain friendly"— consistently points in the direction of the social and relational base of lasting, deep, and meaningful learning. More to the point, climate counts for a great deal; indeed, the wisdom of the character education movement was in recognizing that children cannot learn—and teachers cannot teach—in toxic environments beset by strong negative emotions such as fear, hatred, anger, resentment, disillusionment, and hopelessness. Yet it would be dishonest to say that these negative emotions are unknown in schools, or at least in significant segments of school populations.

The point must be made that there is a synergistic, perhaps even symbiotic, relationship between school staff and student morale and character. The educational mantra of the early 21st century, "No child shall be left behind," reflects a truth that schools are not equally effective for all students. But even as educators are still figuring out the challenges of educating all groups of students, schools still can be places in which students feel accepted, cared about, safe, and valued. As this book proves, we already know a great deal about how to create a high EQ school. Many examples of high EQ schools exist, and their description is the main point of this book.

WHO SHOULD READ THIS BOOK AND WHY

This book is addressed to those who are concerned about building schools as communities. It is intended to show educators how to meet academic standards and how to have schools that are safe and that prepare students to understand the foundation of our system of democracy and participate in its workings. This book is for those who want their schools to change and to be different and better.

Those who learn through case examples can also use this book. It is based on examples from practice that are excellent but also attainable. These schools are not one-time-only projects, but enduring efforts. This book should therefore be of particular interest to educational administrators, curriculum coordinators, superintendents, school board members, parents, and those in college and university programs whose mission includes the preparation of educational leaders.

Also included in the audience for this book are the many professionals whose jobs relate to the climate and character of the schools. These are school psychologists, professional school counselors, substance abuse coordinators, health educators, disciplinarians, student–family support personnel, and other school consultants.

The design of the book is meant to inspire those in a position to influence schoolwide change to make the necessary efforts. It is not a "how-to-do-it" manual because that is not what our readers need at this point. Many people seem to be poised on the sidelines of school change, waiting for a "push" to get into the "game." Sometimes crises of school violence and substance abuse provide the necessary push, but crisis as the catalyst for systematic schoolwide change works against long-term success.

We believe that many of the obstacles to social–emotional learning and EQ (SEL/EQ) are not genuine. As the inspiring examples in this book show, where there is a will, there is a way. Where there is no will to do what is educationally and developmentally sound, children suffer, and we need to label that suffering accurately rather than allow the language of obfuscation to take hold.

This entire book is a testimony to possibility and actuality and must be used to reverse the usual arguments. We must not listen to those on the sidelines who say, "How can we afford to bring SEL into our schools when we have so much to do?"; instead, let us reply with the challenge, "How can you *not* bring SEL into your schools when we see how essential it is for children to become knowledgeable, responsible, nonviolent, and caring?" If not us, then who? If not now, then when? Every reader is "us," and the time is now.

OVERVIEW OF THE BOOK

The text is divided into three parts: (I) Why Schools Must Address EQ and IQ to Be Successful, (II) Creating Learning Communities by Enhancing Schools' SEL and EQ: Examples From Practice, and (III) Making It Happen in Your School: Implementation Guidelines. The editors provide context and a framework for understanding in the introduction to each part.

The book's first in-depth chapter is by James Comer. Dr. Comer's School Development Program has been in operation for more than 30 years and is a presence in approximately

750 schools in all parts of the United States. The impact of his work on urban schools has been particularly powerful. Comer has seen educational fads come and go, but he remains firmly convinced that attending to the social and emotional needs of children is essential for their academic and life success. He places the responsibility for catalyzing the integration of EQ and IQ in schools of character squarely in the court of educational leaders, community leaders, and schools of education. He provides compelling reasons for emphasizing EQ and clear-sighted guiding wisdom for making it happen in schools.

The need to have initiatives in schools that are coordinated, and not merely reactive to the crisis of the moment, is addressed by Mary Utne O'Brien, Roger P. Weissberg, and Timothy P. Shriver, all leaders of CASEL, the Collaborative for Academic, Social, and Emotional Learning. Marcia Knoll and Janet Patti then outline the ways in which EQ contributes to and is essential for academic achievement. They make cogent points about how the attainment of academic standards requires a school building that is focused on learning, and on the joy of learning. Alan Blankstein's chapter provides school administrators with a perspective on how to introduce EQ to teachers and schools. The work he describes represents a collaborative effort across a wide range of experts in the field of social and emotional learning to create a training tool that conveys a common set of principles for blending academics and social–emotional skills. Ronald S. Brandt concludes with a readable discussion of how brain research strongly supports the essential role of social–emotional learning and EQ in school success.

Part II presents examples from practice, written in a way that we hope will touch readers' emotions as well as their intellects. The editors' introduction outlines the range of ways in which EQ has established a foothold in schools in the United States and around the world. The contributions emphasize anecdotes that help readers see the way in which EQ adds tremendous synergy to efforts that might seem adequate at present. Although a variety of approaches to having EQ + IQ in schools are presented, the common denominator is readily apparent: Schools that add EQ to IQ get education with great enthusiasm.

Chapters 6 and 7 reflect the stellar work of Linda Lantieri and the Resolving Conflict Creatively Program and that of Sharon Rose Powell and Margo Ross, directors of the Princeton Center for

Leadership Training. Lantieri shows how she has helped transform the climate of schools by focusing on how they address conflict among students. The intellectual and emotional journey that schools take as they change the way students relate to one another ultimately changes all other relationships in the building, and this leads to a much more EQ-friendly way of teaching than was usually in place earlier. Powell and Ross share their experiences with another approach, that of focusing first on how the adults in the building interact and experience their own sense of community. They illustrate how this starting point also reaches into the relationships between adults and students and among students, eventually filtering into a more respectful and intellectually open approach to teaching and learning.

Approaches to creating entire schools as learning communities follow next. Catherine Lewis, Marilyn Watson, and Eric Schaps present the way in which their Child Development Project has given rise to new methods for creating communities in schools and positively raising the levels of social–emotional and academic accomplishment. Norris Haynes then shares the working principles of Comer's School Development Program, further amplifying the principles that Dr. Comer outlined in our first chapter.

Two other whole-school approaches follow next, directed toward more difficult student populations. The team of Mindy Cohen, Bruce Ettinger, and Terry O'Donnell from The Children's Institute describes how they have been able to create an extraordinary learning environment for special education students through the use of SEL/EQ as an organizing framework. Frank Wallace then shows how EQ has guided the entire structure of the private North Country School, opening students who previously had been quite closed off to academic learning. The principles he articulates are of great generalizability even for those not in a private school.

Finally, Chana Shadmi and Bilha Noy show how an entire nation, Israel, has moved concertedly and quickly to bring SEL/EQ and IQ into its schools. The example has great salience because Israeli education is centralized and structured like a school district. The procedures used to create coherence at a national level have relevance to administrators at regional and local levels who are trying to balance competing priorities, put appropriate curricula in place, and meet diverse needs for direct service, prevention, and social–emotional skill enhancement, while also improving academics. These procedures involve a range of disciplines and forces in the community. Israeli educators have been mobilized to meet these challenges because they realize that in times of crisis, the dual focus on EQ and IQ provides a particularly valuable source of stability. Their lessons have particular relevance for those of us in the United States following the attacks of September 11, 2001.

Part III begins with some distilled wisdom from looking at hundreds of schools—at elementary, middle, and high school levels—that have implemented SEL/EQ approaches over nearly two decades. The editors' introduction also points to Resource B, where resources to support implementation efforts are provided.

Chapter contributions come from three approaches to EQ work in schools that have been implemented successfully thousands of times. Linda Lantieri describes how to bring heart and spirit into schools in ways that increase children's thirst for learning. Linda Bruene Butler, Jeffrey Kress, and Jacqueline Norris draw from their years of experience with the Social Decision Making/Social Problem Solving Program to help administrators understand what is necessary to bring EQ efforts into schools in ways that last. Carol Apacki draws from her vast experience with the programs of Lions-Quest International and shares useful vignettes from places that have brought EQ in without sacrificing IQ. From those stories and related experiences and data, Apacki offers a set of guidelines for administrators as they prepare to implement SEL/EQ into one school, several schools, or an entire school district. Indeed, the chapters in this section share the common denominator of describing how differing SEL/EQ approaches based on a set of shared theoretical principles can be successfully brought into schools in ways that contribute meaningfully to the character and success of those schools.

REFERENCES

Elias, M. J. (2001). Prepare children for the tests of life, not a life of tests. *Education Week, 21*(4), 40.

Goleman, D. (1995). *Emotional intelligence: Why it can matter more than IQ.* New York: Bantam.

Acknowledgments

The editors express appreciation to the many individuals who dedicate their lives in the service of children. These include our contributors and all those members of the teams within which they work, but also others too numerous to name. Some of these persons are known to us, many are not. But what is most important is that children are touched positively by their efforts. Our field needs this kind of continued inspiration and "walking the talk."

We also want to extend thanks to the Fetzer Institute, which provided initial funding to convene many of the contributors and begin the process of sharing and collaboration that has brought such vitality and realism to the chapters herein. Thanks also to the Collaborative for Academic, Social, and Emotional Learning (www.CASEL.org), which has taken as its mission the development of children's social–emotional competencies and the capacity of schools, parents, and communities to support that development. CASEL has leant material, logistical, technical, and moral support essential to the completion of this volume. CASEL also will continue to serve as a catalyst for follow-through of the work that might be sparked as readers see new possibilities for their schools.

Finally, thanks to a wonderful team at Corwin Press. Foremost is our outstanding, creative editor, Faye Zucker, who has been a guiding light throughout this project. Elizabeth Budd provided insightful, sharp, and prompt copyediting. Gracia Alkema has expressed great confidence and belief in the authors' work, has urged the writing of a book like this for years, and has cheered its evolution and completion. We also salute the rest of the Corwin team, including those who designed our wonderful book cover and the overall look and feel of the volume.

INDIVIDUAL ACKNOWLEDGMENTS

I would like to thank Roger Weissberg, Shelley Berman, Janet Patti, Marcia Knoll, Linda Lantieri, Tim Shriver, Eileen Rockefeller Growalt, and Joe Zins of CASEL for educating me a great deal about leadership. Similarly, Bernie Novick, Tom Schuyler, Herb Green, Larry Leverett, Ray Pasi, Bruce Ettinger, and Tony Bencivenga have served as role models and mentors for me in the area of educational administration and leadership. Finally, I must thank my wife, Ellen, and daughters Sara Elizabeth and Samara Alexandra, for their unwavering support for my work on this book and related projects . . . and for letting me use the computer.—M.J.E.

I am most grateful to Maurice Elias, who has advised and encouraged me since I first met him when I was an undergraduate student. Years later, I continue to be inspired by his energy, vision, and dedication to children. I could never thank my parents, Lucille and Nick, enough. They have loved me, encouraged me, and expressed faith in me as long as I can remember. Thank you to the children I have worked with, especially at Children's Village and Monroe Schools. They have taught me well and remain in my heart. Thanks to a cherished Brookside School colleague, Sue Krumm, whose creativity, enthusiasm, and commitment to children set a standard I strive to meet. Finally, thanks to my husband Colin Hussey, who has taught me to be open to the possibilities. His love and support mean more than I can express. —C.S.H.

I would like to extend my thanks to John, my husband, for listening, and to Thomas Nelson, University of the Pacific, and Laura Frey, East Carolina University, for providing helpful suggestions. —H. B. A.

The Publisher gratefully acknowledges the contributions of the following reviewers:

- Michael Ben-Avie, Associate Research Scientist, Yale Child Study Center, New Haven, CT
- Joan Commons, Academic Coordinator, CREATE, University of California, San Diego, CA
- Mimi Gilman, Educational Technology Consultant, Adjunct Professor, Lesley University, Saratoga, NY
- Launa Ellison, Minneapolis Public Schools, MN

About the Editors

Maurice J. Elias, Ph.D., is Professor of Psychology and Coordinator of the Internship Program in Applied, School, and Community Psychology at Rutgers University, Livingston Campus (Piscataway, NJ). He is also Coordinator of the Leadership Team for the Collaborative for Academic, Social, and Emotional Learning (CASEL) and Co-Chair of the CASEL Work Group for Educator Preparation and Leadership for SEL Implementation. His recent books about social and emotional learning include *Social Problem Solving Interventions in the Schools* (2001), *Raising Emotionally Intelligent Teenagers* (2002), *Emotionally Intelligent Parenting: How to Raise a Self-Disciplined, Responsible, Socially Skilled Child* (2000), and *Promoting Social and Emotional Learning: Guidelines for Educators* (1997). He may be reached at MJERU @aol.com and through the Web at *www.EQParenting.com* and *www. casel.org.*

Harriett Arnold, Ed.D., is Associate Professor and Director of the Single Subject Credential Program at the University of the Pacific, Stockton, California, and Facilitator of the Network for Research on Affective Factors in Learning, a special interest group of educators interested in the importance of emotions and learning, funded by the Association of Supervision and Curriculum Development (ASCD). A veteran educator, she has served as an elementary school teacher, secondary administrator, elementary school principal, director of personnel and staff development, and international consultant. Dr. Arnold received an M.Ed. with emphasis in reading from San Jose

State University and a doctorate from the University of San Francisco in curriculum and instruction. She is a member of several professional associations, including ASCD, California ASCD, Association of California School Administrators, California Council on the Education of Teachers, and Phi Delta Kappa. Her publications include numerous articles with an emphasis in curriculum, instruction and the role of emotions in learning; she has also authored the books *Antioch: A Place of Christians* and *Succeeding in the Secondary Classroom: Strategies for Teachers*, the latter of which focuses on beginning teachers. She may be reached at *harnold@uop.edu*.

Cynthia Steiger Hussey, Psy.D., is employed as a School Psychologist by the Monroe Township (New Jersey) Board of Education. She is a member of the American Psychological Association (APA), APA Division 16, the New Jersey Association of School Psychologists, the National Education Association, and the New Jersey Education Association. She is a graduate of Douglass College, Rutgers University, and the Graduate School of Applied and Professional Psychology, Rutgers University. As a graduate student, Dr. Hussey was chosen as a recipient of a Douglass College Alumnae Fellowship. Her dissertation was awarded the graduate school's Cyril Franks Award for excellence in research. She is a member of Psi Chi and Phi Beta Kappa. Her publications include work on the Coping Scale for Children and Youth with David Brodzinsky in the *Journal of Applied Developmental Psychology* and work on special education needs of adopted youth, published in the *Journal of Learning Disabilities.* In her current position, her duties include consulting with teachers, conducting psychological evaluations, providing individual and group counseling, and participation on the school crisis management team.

About the Contributors

Carol Apacki is currently a consultant with Quest International, an initiative of the International Youth Foundation. She has been closely involved in both the development and implementation of Lions-Quest K–12 programs. She also is the author of the *Energize!* book of cooperative games. Prior to her work with Quest International, she served in the Peace Corps in Thailand, taught high school social studies, and worked in teacher education at Denison University. She may be reached at *carolapacki@cswebmail.com*.

Alan Blankstein is founder and president of the HOPE Foundation (Harnessing Optimism and Potential through Education), the mission of which is to develop and connect courageous leaders who collaboratively reshape the culture of school communities to enhance achievement and improve the lives of all children. This takes place through national summits, regional conferences, the National Instructional Leaders Network, and long-term staff development in schools throughout North America. He formerly headed the National Educational Service (NES), which he founded in 1987 and directed for 12 years. He has published award-winning books and video programs, including *Reclaiming Youth At Risk* and *Discipline with Dignity*. He has authored scores of articles in *Educational Leadership*, *The School Administrator*, *Executive Educator*, and *Reaching Today's Youth*, for which he also served as Senior Editor. He is the coauthor of the Reaching Today's Youth curriculum with Rick DuFour and producer of PBS and the C-Span productions from the series *Breaking the Cycle of*

Violence and *Creating Learning Organizations,* which featured international leaders from business, education, and government. Drawing on his own experiences as a former "high-risk" youth in New York, he speaks internationally on how to connect with young people and create high-performing school communities that provide discouraged staff and students with a sense of hope.

Ronald S. Brandt is Executive Editor Emeritus of *Educational Leadership* and other publications of the Association for Supervision and Curriculum Development. He is the author of *Powerful Learning* (1998) and editor of *Assessing Student Learning* (1998) and *Education in a New Era* (2000). His articles have appeared in *Principal, Phi Delta Kappan, Education Week,* and *Leadership News* of the American Association of School Administrators. He currently holds an adjunct appointment as Senior Research Associate to the National Study of School Evaluation, Schaumburg, Illinois. He holds a doctorate from the University of Minnesota.

Linda Bruene Butler, M.Ed., is Clinical Administrator and Director of the Social Decision Making/Problem Solving Program, at the Behavioral Research and Training Institute, University Behavioral HealthCare, University of Medicine and Dentistry of New Jersey. Her research interests include networking schools with advanced level SEL programming and exploring ways that distance learning and technology can promote professional development, training, and technical assistance to schools and represent a component of college course work for preservice educators.

Mindy Cohen, MA, CADC, is a licensed Professional Counselor and Rehabilitation Counselor, a Certified Alcohol and Drug Counselor, Certified Prevention Specialist, Certified American Red Cross Mental Health Disaster Worker, a Psychotherapist Diplomate, and a Nationally Certified School Psychologist. Over the past two decades, Cohen has provided myriad professional services and earned many special awards in her field. She served as the District Crisis Psychologist, Substance Awareness Coordinator and Acting Principal for the Livingston, New Jersey, Board of Education. She was one of the first professionals to be certified by the University of

Medicine and Dentistry of New Jersey's Social Decision Making/Social Problem Solving Program as an SPS Trainer of Trainers. She has written numerous professional articles and is the author of *Thin Kids* (1985). In addition, she has served as a consultant, presenter, and trainer for various organizations including The Children's Institute and Jewish Education Association.

James P. Comer, M.D., is Maurice Falk Professor of Child Psychiatry at the Yale University Child Study Center and Associate Dean of the Yale University School of Medicine. Comer is the Founder of the Yale School Development Program. His books include *Maggie's American Dream: The Life and Times of a Black Family; Waiting for a Miracle: Why Schools Can't Solve Our Problems and How We Can; Rallying the Whole Village: The Comer Process for Reforming Education;* and *Child by Child: The Comer Process for Change in Education.*

Bruce A. Ettinger, Ed.D., has been the Executive Director of The Children's Institute, a widely recognized private special education school, for the past 21 years. He has expertise working with children who have emotional, behavioral, and learning disabilities; attention-deficit disorders; autism; and pervasive developmental delays; and with implementing innovative programs promoting social skills. He has assumed leadership roles in a number of organizations serving the disabled and serves as a speaker and consultant.

Norris M. Haynes, Ph.D., is Professor in the Counseling and School Psychology Department of Southern Connecticut State University and Director of its Center for School Action Research. He is also Associate Clinical Professor at the Yale University Child Study Center. His research interests include a focus on school climate factors and mental health interventions in promoting students' social and emotional development, motivation, self-concept, learning, and achievement. His publications include the books *Rallying the Whole Village: The Comer Process for Reforming Education* and *Child by Child: The Comer Process for Change in Education.*

Marcia Knoll, Ed.D., began her career in education as a teacher and administrator in the New York City Public

Schools and on Long Island. She is currently Associate Professor of Educational Administration and Supervision at Hunter College of CUNY. She has held memberships in the Professional Standards Board, the National Council for Accreditation of Teacher Education Institutions Board of Examiners; consulted to Regional Labs, state education departments, county and school districts; and is Past President of Association for Supervision and Curriculum Development. Her most recent book is *Administrator's Guide to Student Achievement and Higher Test Scores* (2002).

Jeffrey S. Kress, Ph.D., is Senior Research Assistant at the William Davidson School of Jewish Education and Adjunct Assistant Professor in the Department of Jewish Education at the Jewish Theological Seminary in New York City. He has worked as a program development specialist at the Social Decision Making/Problem Solving Program at the Behavioral Research and Training Institute at University Behavioral HealthCare, University of Medicine and Dentistry of New Jersey, where he was involved in training and consultation regarding a research-validated social skills and problem-solving curriculum.

Linda Lantieri has more than 30 years of experience in education as a teacher, administrator, and college faculty member. She is founding director of the Resolving Conflict Creatively Program of Educators for Social Responsibility and Director of the New York/Metro Satellite Office of the Collaborative for Academic, Social, and Emotional Learning (*www.CASEL. org*). Lantieri is coauthor of *Waging Peace in Our Schools* (1996) and editor of *Schools With Spirit: Nurturing the Inner Lives of Children and Teachers* (2001). She may be reached at *llantieri@ rccp.org*.

Catherine Lewis, Ph.D., is a member of the Education Department at Mills College in Oakland, CA. Her award-winning book *Educating Hearts and Minds: Reflections on Japanese Preschool and Elementary Education* focuses on how Japanese teachers foster social and academic development simultaneously. She directed formative research on the Child Development Project and currently directs a

National Science Foundation-funded study of instructional improvement in Japan that highlights teacher-led "lesson study" (*www.lessonresearch.net*).

Jacqueline Norris, Ed.D., is an educator with more than 30 years of experience in New Jersey schools. She has taught at the elementary and secondary levels, been both a school- and district-level administrator, and is presently a Professor of Education at the College of New Jersey. As Assistant Superintendent, she implemented SEL in a district and now works to integrate the skills of SEL into teacher education at the college level.

Bilha Noy, Ph.D., is Head of the Counseling and School Psychology Service within the Ministry of Education of Israel. She has served as head of counseling service in a comprehensive school and as team leader in a school for senior workers in education. She established the Open Line for Children and has published in the areas of children's rights, parent–school relationships, and violence prevention.

Mary Utne O'Brien, Ph.D., is Associate Director of the Collaborative for Academic, Social, and Emotional Learning, where she directs efforts to form a network of national and regional organizations to provide training and support to leaders who champion SEL policy and practice. She works with educational leaders to identify the skills, information, and resources they need to implement effective SEL programming. O'Brien also works with other researchers and experienced practitioners to identify effective strategies for the implementation, monitoring, and assessment of SEL practice.

Therese O'Donnell, M.A., has been Principal of The Children's Institute for the past 16 years. She is also a speech pathologist, has expertise working with children with a wide range of disabilities, and serves as a consultant and speaker.

Janet Patti, Ed.D., worked for more than 25 years as a teacher, counselor, and administrator in the public school systems of New York City and San Diego. She is Associate Professor and Coordinator of the Educational Administration and Supervision Program at Hunter College. She is also a member of the CASEL

Leadership Team, coauthor of *Waging Peace in Our Schools* (1996), a lead trainer for Educators for Social Responsibility's Don't Laugh at Me Program, and is internationally recognized in the fields of conflict resolution, intergroup relations, and educational leadership.

Sharon Rose Powell, Ed.D., is the founding president of the Princeton Center for Leadership Training, a nonprofit organization with a 20-year record of delivering leadership development programs and services in schools and communities. Powell is a New Jersey Licensed Psychologist and Marriage and Family Therapist and a Contributing Faculty member at the Graduate School of Applied and Professional Psychology at Rutgers University.

Margo Ross, Psy.D., is Director of New Jersey Peer to Peer (NJPTP) at the Princeton Center for Leadership Training. NJPTP is a statewide, youth leadership development program for middle schools focused on substance abuse prevention and social and emotional skill development. She is a Certified School Psychologist in New Jersey.

Eric Schaps is founder and president of the Developmental Studies Center in Oakland, CA, a nonprofit organization that specializes in designing educational programs and evaluating their effects on children's academic, ethical, social, and emotional development. He is the author of three books and 60 chapters and articles on school improvement, prevention of problem behaviors, prosocial development, and program evaluation.

Chana Shadmi is associated with the Israel Psychological and Counseling Services division of the Israeli Ministry of Education in Jerusalem, and developed the "Windows" curriculam.

Timothy P. Shriver, Ph.D., is President and Chief Executive Officer of Special Olympics. In that capacity, he serves more than one million Special Olympics athletes and their families in 150 countries worldwide. Before joining Special Olympics in 1995, Shriver launched and was supervisor of the New Haven, CT, Public Schools' Social Development Project, the country's most noted school-based project focused on preventing substance abuse, violence, dropout, and teen pregnancy. Before launching the project, Shriver was a teacher in the New Haven public schools and a teacher and counselor in the University of Connecticut's Upward Bound program. He has written extensively on effective school-based prevention programming and has coauthored several publications, including *Promoting Social & Emotional Learning: Guidelines for Educators* (1997). In recent years, he has applied his educational interests to film. He is the coproducer of DreamWorks Studios' 1997 release *Amistad* and Disney Studios' 2000 release *The Loretta Claiborne Story*.

Frank Wallace has worked with children and teachers for 40 years. As Headmaster of Colorado Academy, he taught a weekly seminar for teachers on child and adolescent development. He has written on childhood and schooling for journals and public radio. Between 1992 and 1999, he was Headmaster of North Country School, the setting for his essay included in this volume. He is the founder and president of Educational Consultants.com. He may be reached at *www.educationalconsultants.com* or at *fwallace@maine.rr.com*.

Marilyn Watson recently retired from the Developmental Studies Center (DSC) in Oakland, CA, where she had been Program Director of the Child Development Project, and headed DSC's work in the area of preservice education. Prior to her work at DSC, Watson was a faculty member in the education department at Mills College in Oakland and the Director of the Mills College Children's School.

Roger Weissberg is a Professor of Psychology and Education at the University of Illinois at Chicago (UIC). He is Executive Director of the Collaborative for Academic, Social, and Emotional Learning (CASEL). He directs UIC's National Institute of Mental Health-funded Prevention Research Training Program in Urban Children's Mental Health. He has received awards for designing, evaluating, and disseminating school-based prevention programs including the Award for Distinguished Contribution of Applications of Psychology to Education and Training from the American Psychological Association.

**CORWIN
PRESS**

The Corwin Press logo—a raven striding across an open book—
represents the happy union of courage and learning. We are a
professional-level publisher of books and journals for K-12
educators, and we are committed to creating and providing
resources that embody these qualities. Corwin's motto is
"Success for All Learners."

PART ONE

Why Schools Must Address EQ and IQ to be Successful

EQ, IQ, and Effective Learning and Citizenship

Maurice J. Elias

Harriett Arnold

Cynthia Steiger Hussey

EMOTIONAL INTELLIGENCE 101: THE BASICS

So what is emotional intelligence? The term itself was coined by Peter Salovey of Yale University and Jack Mayer of the University of New Hampshire while they were researching factors important to functioning well in society (Mayer & Salovey, 1997). But it was Daniel Goleman's (1995) book *Emotional Intelligence* that brought this idea to the general public in the United States and worldwide.

A good way to understand emotional intelligence is to take note of its shorthand acronym: "EQ." EQ complements the acronym IQ, which has come to be recognized as signifying academic achievement, typically of a cognitive nature. If IQ represents the intellectual raw material of student success, EQ is the set of social–emotional skills that enables intellect to turn into action and accomplishment.

Without EQ, IQ consists more of potential than actuality. It is confined more to performance on certain kinds of tests than to expression in the many tests of everyday life in school, at home, at the workplace, in the community. EQ is the missing piece in true reform of education and preparation of students for academic and life success. Schools that see as their mission the joint and synergistic development of EQ + IQ must become the standard of education. Those who lead such schools know this well. Those who aspire to lead such schools are visionaries who are ready to prepare students for the complexities of life in the 21st century and beyond.

Identifying Core Characteristics of EQ

There are many definitions of emotional intelligence, and research continues to refine the nuances of this concept. CASEL, the Collaborative for Academic, Social, and Emotional Learning (www.CASEL.org), continues to play a prominent role in monitoring and articulating these changes, especially through its ongoing process of reviewing EQ-related programs to determine their features and adequacy. However, it is useful to understand EQ as expressed by Daniel Goleman in *Emotional Intelligence* because this is the most widespread shared terminology in use.

1. Self-Awareness: the ability to recognize feelings as they occur in real-life situations

2. Management and Self-Regulation of Emotions: being able to cope with strong feelings so as not to be overwhelmed and paralyzed by them

3. Self-Motivation and Performance: being goal-oriented and able to channel emotions toward desired outcomes

4. Empathy and Perspective Taking: being able to recognize emotions in others and to understand others' point of view

5. Social Skills: the ability to handle a range of social relationships

Resource A shows a more detailed elaboration of these areas and provides formats for assessing specific social and emotional learning (SEL) and EQ skills in oneself and in one's students.

EQ, or skills for social and emotional learning, are therefore those skills that underlie the following elements of everyday classroom and school life:

- Communicating effectively
- Participating actively, genuinely, and cooperatively in group work
- Expressing and regulating emotions and impulses appropriately
- Resolving conflicts thoughtfully and nonviolently
- Living a life of sound character
- Bringing a reflective, learning-to-learn approach to all domains of life

EQ in Schools

Can there be true academic and social success without these types of skills? When the Association for Supervision and Curriculum Development (ASCD) ran articles in *Educational Leadership* on effective middle schools, the common denominator among the schools was that they had systematic procedures in place for addressing children's social and emotional skills. There were schoolwide mentoring programs, group guidance and advisory periods, modifications of the usual discipline systems, and classroom programs that allowed time for group problem solving and team building. Of course, they had sound academic programs and competent teachers and administrators, but other schools had these features as well. It was the social and emotional learning component that distinguished them.

WHY EDUCATORS MUST CARE ABOUT SOCIAL AND EMOTIONAL LEARNING AND EMOTIONAL INTELLIGENCE (SEL/EQ)

Reason 1: Academic Learning and Performance Are Linked to Social and Emotional Skill Development

When one looks carefully at the resilience literature and other examples of cases in which success occurs in unexpected circumstances and failure under favorable conditions, one can find "the missing piece": The very nature of school-based learning is relational, and social and emotional skills are essential for building and sustaining learning relationships of the kind needed for academic success, citizenship, a civilized and nonviolent classroom, and effective inclusive education.

The missing piece in the process of civilizing and humanizing our children, without doubt, is social and emotional learning. Any protestations that this province is outside and separate from the domain of the school is inaccurate, harmful, and dooms us to continued frustration and Herculean efforts at damage control and repair. Meanwhile, the roster of social casualties will grow ever larger.

Sylwester (1995) documented the way in which memory is event coded, linked to social and emotional situations, and how the latter are integral parts of larger units of memory that make up what people learn and retain—including and especially what takes place in the classroom. Among the key points that show the centrality of social and emotional learning are the following:

> We know emotion is very important to the educative process because it drives attention, which drives learning and memory. We've never really understood emotion, however, and so don't know how to regulate it in school-beyond defining too much or too little of it as misbehavior and relegating most of it to the arts, PE, recess, and the extracurricular program. (p. 72)
>
> Our emotions allow us to assemble life-saving information very quickly, and thus to bypass the extended conscious and rational deliberation of a potential threat. . . . Thus, stereotyped information can lead to irrational fears

and to prejudicial and foolish behaviors that we may later regret when we get more detailed and objective information from the slower cortical analysis. (p. 73)

By separating emotion from logic and reason in the classroom, we've simplified school management and evaluation, but we've also then separated two sides of one coin—and lost something important in the process. It's impossible to separate emotion from the other important activities of life. Don't try. . . . Scientists have now replaced this duality with an integrated body/brain system. (p. 75)

The development of a long-term memory emerges out of an ill-understood, often conscious decision that elements of the current situation are emotionally significant and will probably reoccur [other memories—including initial skill learning—are believed to be linked to and encoded in terms of their social and emotional context]. (pp. 93–94)

Most of our brain's neural networks process the complex interactions that lead to the analysis and solution of problems. (p. 106)

Three broad areas of organizing this information in our brain are described as temporal, spatial, and personal, the latter of which comprises intra and interpersonal awareness.

We are a social organism, depending on others for many important things in life. (p. 114)

It's difficult to think of linguistic, musical, and interpersonal intelligence out of the context of social and cooperative activity, and the other four forms of intelligence are likewise principally social in normal practice. (p. 117)

Sylwester (1995) outlined six areas in which emotional and social learning must come together for the benefit of children and schools.

- Accepting and controlling our emotions
- Using metacognitive activities

- Using activities that promote social interaction
- Using activities that provide an emotional context
- Avoiding intense emotional stress in school
- Recognizing the relationship between emotions and health (pp. 75–77)

The skills and areas that Sylwester identified mirror the skills identified by Goleman (1995) and by Mayer and Salovey (1997) as essential for EQ or "emotional literacy" and by CASEL (Elias, Zins, Weissberg, & Associates, 1997) as the basis of programs and other efforts to promote social and emotional learning.

Reason 2: Social and Emotional Skills Are Essential Skills for Citizenship in a Democracy—in Classrooms, Schools, Families, Workplaces, Teams, and Communities

Democracy was under direct attack on September 11, 2001. As is now clear, the defense of freedom is not purely a military matter. Our freedom depends on an informed citizenry exercising sound judgment and stepping up to help others in need. It depends on skilled social and civic participation and protection of civil liberties from assaults from abroad and within.

Beane and Apple (1995) illustrated how EQ truly connects diverse aspects of learning and schooling with life skills and everyday interpersonal decision making to foster a synergy that can be put into place more systematically than currently occurs.

> To say that democracy rests on the consent of the governed is almost a cliche, but in a democratic school, it is true that all of those directly involved in the school, including young people, have the right to participate in the process of decision making. . . . In classrooms, young people and teachers engage in collaborative planning, reaching decisions that respond to the concerns, aspirations, and interests of both. (p. 9)
>
> The democratic way of life engages the creative process of seeking ways to extend and expand the values of democracy. This process, however, is not simply an anticipatory conversation about just anything. Rather, it is

directed toward intelligent and reflective consideration of problems, events, and issues that arise in the course of our collective lives. (p. 16)

The New Jersey Core Curriculum Standards recognizes the central place of social and emotional skills in the context of cross-setting workplace skills and as the centerpiece of comprehensive health education. The curriculum standards of other states, as well, contain a number of implicit and explicit SEL/EQ connections (Norris & Kress, 2000). When one delineates standards for skills that children must have to be considered well educated, it is no longer responsible to omit SEL/EQ from any such list.

Reason 3: Promoting EQ + IQ Is an Essential Task for Educational Leaders

Educators need to see more than how social and emotional learning is critical to the process of civilizing, humanizing, and educating students. The very nature of school-based learning is relational. Social and emotional learning is essential for building and sustaining learning relationships of the kind needed for academic success, citizenship, a civilized and nonviolent classroom, and effective inclusive education. Educational leaders must take a leading role in making the case that many of the problems in the schools are the result of social and emotional debilitation that children have suffered and continue to suffer.

The basic skills of social and emotional learning are necessary for students to be able to take full advantage of their biological equipment and social legacy and heritage. As schools provide the conditions that allow even the most "at-risk" students to become engaged in the learning process, new possibilities open up and new life trajectories are made available to them. Resilience research makes clear that in even the worst conditions within our inner cities, one can still find some children emerging in positive ways. In these cases, expect to find that social and emotional learning was provided to such children by one or two caring people, often those in their schools.

Academic and social success should not be the product of good fortune or of privileged upbringing; it is based on conditions that are created in the lives of young people. "EQ + IQ" provides administrators with background, examples, and guidelines to foster these conditions in schools—programmatically and systematically—so that their existence for all children is left less to chance than currently is the case.

The chapters that follow in Part I provide essential background, evidence, and perspective for understanding the relationship of EQ and IQ. With Part I as a base, the examples of how EQ has been brought into schools and districts presented in Part II may be more deeply understood, and the principles that underlie them may become more apparent, allowing application to diverse settings.

REFERENCES

Beane, J. A., & Apple, M. W. (1995). The case for democratic schools. In M. W. Apple & J. A. Beane (Eds.), *Democratic schools* (pp. 1–25). Alexandria, VA: Association for Supervision and Curriculum Development.

Elias, M. J., Zins, J., Weissberg, R. P., & Associates. (1997). *Promoting social and emotional learning: Guidelines for educators.* Alexandria, VA: Association for Supervision and Curriculum Development.

Goleman, D. (1995). *Emotional intelligence.* New York: Bantam.

Mayer, J. D., & Salovey, P. (1997). What is emotional intelligence? In J. D. Mayer & P. Salovey (Eds.), *Emotional development and emotional intelligence* (pp. 3–31). New York: Basic Books.

Norris, J., & Kress, J. S. (2000). Reframing the standards vs. social and emotional learning debate: A case study. *The Fourth R, 91*(2), 7–10.

Sylwester, R. (1995). *A celebration of neurons: An educator's guide to the human brain.* Alexandria, VA: Association for Supervision and Curriculum Development.

CHAPTER ONE

Transforming the Lives of Children

James P. Comer

Until I became involved in schools, I didn't understand that children need to form emotional bonds with their teachers and see healthy social relationships among the adults in their lives to function well in school. Our first year in two New Haven, Connecticut, schools was so chaotic that I began to reflect on my own childhood experiences to try to figure out what kind of environment had to be created so that the students would be able to learn and develop well.

When I was in school, I often received better treatment than other students of the same racial and socioeconomic background. There was something about coming from a solid family, something about my father's reliability, and something about all those times my mother would go to the school that resulted in the teachers treating me differently. My interest in the emotional aspects of learning perhaps stems from my realization even then that this treatment was helpful to me.

I didn't really understand the how and the why of it until many years later when I became involved in schools in 1968 when the Yale Child Study Center and the New Haven Public Schools formed a partnership. As the head of the team from the Yale Child Study Center, I observed that the students were not the only ones who had trouble interacting with school personnel. There were also difficulties in the relationships between teachers and administrators and among custodians, staff, and parents.

My childhood experiences and my training in child development had taught me that all those people needed to work together to support the healthy development of children. At the time, however, school reform experts, schools of education, school people, and policymakers were all talking about cognitive factors, linguistic factors, intellectual factors, cognitive–linguistic factors, linguistic–intellectual factors, and so forth. No one was talking about social–emotional factors. Nobody was talking about relationships.

Even the literature on child development didn't offer much insight because at the time it focused almost entirely on parents. I realized that one of the reasons why children were not functioning well in school was because of difficult relationships between parents and school staff. The students were taking advantage of tensions between the teachers and the parents. They were playing one against the other. Although the research literature on child development wasn't too helpful, my training in child development showed me that children need to see their parents respected by the school staff. They need to see all the adults in their lives working together. For children to learn how to regulate their own emotions appropriately, they need to see adults doing so in their interactions.

SCHOOLS WHERE ADULTS WORK TOGETHER TO SUPPORT CHILD DEVELOPMENT AND LEARNING

Today the School Development Program (SDP) helps schools throughout the country implement a process that helps schools recreate community and thereby promote the learning and development of students.

As I describe the process, it might sound as if we knew from the beginning what we needed to do, but in fact a lot of what we did was just to survive. The beginning was so chaotic that we were almost thrown out of the schools at the end of the first year! The chaos stemmed, in part, from a focus on everything but what the kids actually needed. People had a lot of plans. They wanted to be creative with the curriculum and they had good ideas about instruction and classroom organization. However, I asked them to start instead by asking the questions that no one else was asking at that time.

- What do children need to function well in school?
- How can adults work together to support child development?
- What kind of school environment must we create to support child development?

The key point I needed to convey was the following: When children are developing well, and when they feel emotionally connected to their school, then children can learn.

Just lecturing teachers and staff about child development wasn't enough. We had to begin by creating structures that allowed parents, teachers, staff, and district administrators to work together. We didn't mandate change (actually, the people in charge had tried to mandate it, but it didn't work). Instead, what we did was create a new conceptual framework and operational structure designed to bring about change gradually. We created a school governance and management mechanism, consisting of three teams, that was representative of all the stakeholders in the building. I turned especially to parents who had been complaining about the school program and who now were invited to join us in our efforts.

THE SCHOOL TEAMS AND THEIR WORK

Our School Planning and Management Team (SPMT) was the team charged with answering the question: "What kind of school do we want?" We knew that we had to be guided by the expectations of the school district central office, but we also knew that we were the experts on the children in our building and the problems they faced. So we pioneered what is known today as site-based management.

Trust

We had to start with basic issues of trust, authority, and communication. Students were acting up and acting out because the school environment didn't support their developmental needs. Parents didn't trust the school because they were used to broken promises and endless parades of new teachers. Teachers cared about their students but didn't know how to set limits with them or how to exercise authority in developmentally appropriate ways. And the teachers came from a culture in which they were supposed to have learned everything already and to know how to do everything. For this reason, they were unable to articulate their own needs for help in managing classroom behavior or in teaching content in areas in which they had not been trained.

Comprehensive Planning

The SPMT took on the role of developing the Comprehensive School Plan, with input from the two other teams (the Parent Team and the Student and Staff Support Team). The Comprehensive School Plan even today is the mechanism by which all the activities in the school are coordinated. Student needs are identified. Staff development is aligned with these identified needs. A way is designed to monitor whether the staff development was effective and whether the identified needs were addressed. All the activities within the school are aligned to promote students' development, including social and emotional development.

In addition to the School Planning and Management Team, we introduced a Parent Team. The parents selected their representatives for the School Planning and Management Team to decide school governance issues. More important, the parents also sponsored school programs to support social–emotional growth—their own and the students'. Parent involvement in SDP schools is about parents supporting the development of all the children in the school, and not just their own children.

We started out calling the Student and Staff Support Team the Mental Health Team because it included all of the helping professionals who often worked separately in schools: the psychologist, social worker, special education teacher, nurse, and so forth. Along the way, we changed the name to the Student and Staff Support Team (SSST), not just to escape the stigma that often accompanies mental health issues, but also in recognition of the team's authentic efforts to change the school's climate and culture.

The SSST supports child development by focusing on prevention—instead of intervention when a problem has already escalated into a major crisis—on the global level and the level of the individual student. We had found that most services provided to children tend to be fragmented and inefficient. For example, we observed seven professionals helping one child, with each one doing his or her piece, and none of them talking to one another. The SSST focuses on global preventive measures because we have found that if the adults create a supportive overall environment in the school, most children do not need mental health services.

Consensus, Collaboration, and No-Fault Problem Solving

For the teams to function well, we teach three relationship guidelines: consensus, collaboration, and no fault. *Consensus* decision making isn't about who's right. It's about what works well for the children. *Collaboration* means that we work together in teams: The principal must not ignore the teams, and the teams must not paralyze the principal. And *no-fault* means that we avoid defensive behaviors and focus instead on solving problems rather than wasting energy on assigning blame for problems.

Creating Community

What we're really doing is re-creating community in schools in ways that allow the children to make healthy emotional attachments. We want the children to create emotional bonds with their teachers and school staff that build on the emotional attachments that they have with their own parents. By keeping the parents actively involved with the work of the schools, the children learn how to imitate, identify with, and internalize the attitudes, values, ways of working, and ways of managing the world that they see modeled all around them. Children in SDP schools learn to talk about consensus, collaboration, and no fault just the way the adults do. They learn the same approach to living together in the school and in the community.

CHILD DEVELOPMENT ALONG MULTIPLE PATHWAYS

The SDP is often described as one of the school reform models. I think we're much more than that. Of course, we want to improve student performance. Yet the SDP is interested in far more than just cognitive development. To understand this point, it is worthwhile to pause for a moment and talk about human functioning.

There are six pathways that are critical for academic learning and effective functioning: cognitive, physical, language, social, psychological, and ethical. The idea of the developmental pathways helps me to organize the many aspects of development in a framework. For example, people talk about self-awareness, self-regulation of emotions, anger management, and so forth. In the way that I conceptualize development, all of these aspects would come under the psychological developmental pathway (originally, this pathway was called psychological–emotional to emphasize the emotional aspects of psychological functioning). Social skills, empathy, and perspective taking involve the social pathway and the cognitive pathway. So the developmental pathways help me to frame all the aspects of development that are involved in emotional intelligence.

SDP schools tend not to use the terms "EQ" and "IQ"—and I worry that those terms may lead us to slip into thinking numbers about social skills and psychoemotional development. I'm not certain that I could name the seven components of "emotional intelligence" or the eight "multiple intelligences" with precision, but I will use the terms EQ and IQ in our schools if I must to convey the point that EQ is just as important as IQ. In fact, I think EQ is more important. We have to begin to look at the elements of EQ—the social, psychological, and ethical pathways—and show that this can also predict school success, perhaps even more so than IQ.

I reported recently on the Samuel Gompers Elementary School in Detroit (Comer, 2001). The school population is 98% poor and Black. Yet in 2000 they had the highest test scores in the fourth grade in the state of Michigan. How did that happen? I believe it happened because the school created a community that supported the students' development along all the pathways. The school community created the conditions that allowed the children to forge emotional attachments to the adults and to the value of schooling.

Activities at the school's daily morning assembly all focus on transmitting to the children a core set of attitudes, values, and beliefs that reinforce confidence and competence.

- The students pledge allegiance to the U.S. flag and sing patriotic songs, but they also salute their own school flag and sing their own school songs.
- The students recognize birthdays every morning, and the school custodians lead that event, thus always modeling and reinforcing the community belief that *everybody* counts.
- The students plan schoolwide projects that help children in countries that are even poorer than inner-city Detroit.
- The students celebrate winning citywide basketball championships, but they also discuss how to manage their disappointment when they lose the championship: They learn how to mourn their losses and then try again.
- They focus on academic achievement every morning by allowing the class with the best test scores for each month to parade the school mascot at the start-of-day assembly.

When the school is organized to promote students' development, children from the lowest socioeconomic population can achieve the best test scores.

TEACHER EDUCATION THAT SUPPORTS CHILD DEVELOPMENT AND LEARNING

Schools of education aren't paying enough attention to child development either. They focus on cognitive–intellectual, linguistic growth, but they forget about social–interactive development, psychoemotional development, ethical development, and physical development. Schools of education must learn to understand social–emotional intelligence before they can teach it meaning-fully, and they must learn to assess levels of development because we know that what we measure in our schools and school districts strongly influences how we teach there.

Schools of education also have to prepare new teachers for the stressful environments they will encounter in real class-rooms in real schools, and this means improving teacher train-ing, field experiences, observation, and supervision. It doesn't do a principal much good to hire a new teacher who earned all A's in college and who looks like a winner during a job interview but who turns out to be an absolute disaster in the classroom. We need to see more professors of education leaving campus to observe their trainees during their fieldwork before we will see the improvements in teacher education that our communi-ties need.

PUBLIC POLICY THAT SUPPORTS CHILD DEVELOPMENT AND LEARNING

Higher test scores are not the only goal of schools, although many political leaders seem to have forgotten that fact these days. Schools face new and continuing challenges in many domains.

Social and Economic Stressors

In addition to the wave of anxiety created when New York's World Trade Center was destroyed in 2001, the extreme social stresses of family and community poverty continue to affect stu-dent performance. A student cannot perform competitively on a standardized test if that student has no light or heat at home because of unpaid utility bills or if that student's parent has just gone to jail. Some of our schools are in neighborhoods where students have to go up to the roof to identify where gangs are hanging out so that the students can figure out how to walk home safely without encountering those gangs.

Pay Inequities

Struggling school districts often work hard to make slow but significant progress, only to be stopped by pay inequities. Hardworking teachers who gain teaching skills and teaching credentials cannot be expected to resist leaving inner-city schools for more comfortable suburban teaching posts that can offer salaries that are $20,000 or $25,000 more per year. The struggling schools lose the skilled teachers just when they attain the high level of competence essential to school improvement, leaving the schools who need skilled teachers the most to plug along with the least experienced teachers or with teachers working out of their fields of competence. Those are consequences of a system under severe economic and social stress.

Untapped Resources

School budgets often talk about cutting out "frills," but look at what we're losing along the way:

- *Creativity.* Students may not always begin with academic success, but students who are allowed to use their creativity can inspire teachers to perceive them differently, and we know that can lead to improved academic performance. Music teachers and art teachers greatly enrich the lives of students, offering a greater intensity of interaction than the regular classroom teacher who is teaching to a state-mandated test.
- *Project-based learning.* Projects that involve teachers, parents, and students interacting with their community teach all kinds of academic, social–interactive, and ethical lessons. A project about the life and times of Jackie Robinson that includes a museum visit, for example, will teach students about segregation, the Civil Rights Movement, asking questions of museum tour guides and listening respectfully to the answers, the practical skills necessary for a bus trip, and the social skills for a stop at a restaurant on the way home.
- *Athletic coaches and arts teachers in the school and in the community.* Not only are athletic coaches trained to teach essential psychomotor skills, they also can model ways to handle feelings and express emotions in intense interactions. The same is true of

art and music teachers. All of these activities help children learn a range of skills involved in performance competencies. Participating in activities such as marching band combines many important pathways to learning. Such people are found not only in the schools. Coaches in leagues such as Pop Warner and Babe Ruth are a tremendously underutilized community resource.

CHARACTER EDUCATION AND SCHOOL SAFETY

The political and business communities want the schools to "teach character," to help the students acquire social skills and improve their psychoemotional development. In fact, schools cannot teach character because it's not an isolated cognitive process. Schools have to create an environment that models and promotes character development, and then they have to allow the children to "catch" character from the behavior of the adults and students around them.

One of our schools had an incident in which a teacher accused a student of having "street smarts." The student reported the insult to his parents, and the father came in to school to confront the teacher: "What right do you have to tell my son that he has street smarts?" The father was especially upset because the family was White and the teacher was African American. It's possible that other parents might have sent this teacher a note of thanks for complimenting their child, but the net result in this case was a series of nonproductive interactions that were not helpful to the teacher, the child, the parent, or the school.

We know that respect for authority is part of character development, but this child had in fact pitted one authority figure in his life against another, and he did that in his own self-defense. The student was never asked about his own responsibility to prevent the problem that led to the original insult, but the student did learn more about manipulating people and beating the system. Nor was the teacher asked about her responsibility for preventing the problem. But because the teacher is a human being, she probably won't be able to go back into the classroom and respond to that child in a more constructive fashion. Thus the school has gained nothing useful from these interactions because the school failed to create an environment in which people can talk together, trust each other, respect each other, and solve problems without blame. The school has failed to model or to promote good character development.

School climate creates the learning environment for character, particularly in the area of school safety and teaching about nonviolence. Here is another school incident to consider: A 9-year-old student had transferred schools four times in one semester and finally was transferred into an SDP school. Someone stepped on his foot, and his dukes went up. He was ready to fight because that was the model he had encountered everywhere else he had been that year and in prior years. But another student saw the fighting stance and said, "Hey, man, we don't do that in this school." And the new student looked around, and sure enough, the facial expression of the nearby teacher and all the other students all echoed the simple statement, "We don't fight in this school."

That environment taught consensus, collaboration, and no-fault problem solving. When the school itself teaches and models consensus, collaboration, and no-fault problem solving, children then become the proud carriers of their school's culture. Now that's a good way to create nonviolent schools. That is a school where emotionally intelligent students can thrive. Those students have social skills, and one of them had the courage and the leadership skill to speak up to stop violence before it began.

EDUCATIONAL LEADERSHIP THAT SUPPORTS CHILD DEVELOPMENT AND LEARNING

Educators are the ones who must keep reminding our political leaders that being successful in life means more than high test scores. Our political leaders have a fascination with high-stakes tests that can be used for gatekeeping functions. And because those tests work so well for privileged populations, our leaders will continue to support them and push them on us. But educational leaders must continue to weaken political arguments about the value of tests.

We cannot document a direct connection between IQ and life success. We must begin to look at the elements of EQ, emotions and feelings, the social–interactive, the psychoemotional, and the ethical pathways, and we must begin to show the connection between those factors and life success.

People with the highest IQs are not the most successful people in our society. Our society must be reminded to value the arts and athletics as well as opportunities for self-expression. That is how we can build smart, safe, emotionally intelligent schools and communities.

REFERENCE

Comer, James P. (2001, April 23). Schools that develop children. *The American Prospect, 12, 7.*

C H A P T E R   T W O

Educational Leadership for Academic, Social, and Emotional Learning

Mary Utne O'Brien

Roger P. Weissberg

Timothy P. Shriver

Educational leaders have always been forced to address social and behavioral problems that find their way, uninvited, into the schools. This is a continuing challenge to which few genuinely effective responses have been developed. In the mid-1990s, we wrote an article for *Education Week* called "No New Wars!" (Shriver & Weissberg, 1996). It opened with a description of the myriad categorical responses to student problems that typified schools at that time. Discrete programs abounded that addressed student drug use, AIDS and pregnancy prevention, poor citizenship, discipline, and other problem behaviors. These problems still abound, and now we can add to the list of "crisis crusades" the programs generated by Columbine and other school shootings, the September 11, 2001, terrorist attack and its after-math, and concerns about the achievement gap and American students' underachievement in general. Educational leaders need to respond to these diverse challenges in a coherent and effective way that recognizes the reality of children and schools, as well as of the society in which we now live.

One approach is the reactive, short-term, categorical "war on the problem" approach that we wrote about in 1996. Given limited time in the curriculum; limited resources to support and sustain planned, ongoing, and coordinated initiatives; limited training supports; and the pressures of testing, it is understandable that educational leaders resort to this response. Nonetheless, it is unlikely to be effective for the following reasons:

- Staff members may work on similar issues without any coordination of expertise or resources.
- Few prevention programs last more than a few years, which is not long enough for improvements to be made.
- There is little developmental or curricular continuity across grade levels and schools.
- Many initiatives are reactive rather than preventive, so that by the time the work is begun, the problem is well out of hand.
- Different programs are frequently aimed at the same children, splitting them into categories of problem behaviors and never addressing the causes underlying the problems in the first place.

Meanwhile, the larger body of students receives little or no attention or help with the challenging developmental issues they face. As a result, new prevention initiatives are met with ambivalence in most schools. School personnel frequently regard problem prevention campaigns with skepticism and frustration, because most have been introduced as a succession of disjointed fads. Fragmentation breeds breakdown, and the school emerges as a hodgepodge of social initiatives with little direction or effectiveness. At the same time, teachers are held more closely accountable than ever before for student performance on standardized tests. To them, these programs seem at best to be tangential to the academic mission; at worst, teachers see them as taking away precious time needed for academic focus. Unfortunately, they have also left undiminished those problems that spurred on the programs.

A NEW STRATEGY IS REQUIRED

It is time for a different strategy. We need not counter each behavior issue that arises with a new categorical initiative that has no place in the structure of the school. Instead, schools can capitalize on what they are already in the business of doing: promoting the personal and social development and well-being of children en route to imparting academic skills and knowledge. They can proactively build comprehensive programs that help children develop academically, socially, and emotionally. We call these social and emotional learning (SEL) programs. As a result of SEL, children become competent in ways that can help them to learn better and to avoid problem behaviors. Such an approach requires leadership that is committed to creating a coherent vision and that will work to marshal the resources and the staff energy and skills needed to realize it.

We begin our description of the SEL approach by making explicit a few assumptions:

1. Virtually all educators and parents want to graduate young people who are knowledgeable, responsible, caring, and healthy.

2. Social and emotional factors are key contributors to producing positive outcomes, including academic performance that measures up to one's potential; positive relationships

with peers and adults; constructive citizenship; coping with stress, challenges, and developmental tasks; and making positive decisions across academic, social, and health domains. They are also key factors in preventing problem outcomes such as drug use, unwanted pregnancy, delinquency, bullying, violence, dropout, truancy, and underachievement.

3. Failure to live up to the potential for positive behavior, as well as rates of problem behaviors, are higher in most schools and communities than we would like.

4. Lack of motivation for achievement; lack of commitment to schooling, family and community; and engagement in problem behaviors co-occur.

5. Many of these issues could be addressed in the context of the same interventions.

6. Most schools are trying to educate knowledgeable, responsible, caring, and healthy students, but all schools could benefit from information and support about the latest advances in science and practice.

SOCIAL AND EMOTIONAL LEARNING: A PROACTIVE ALTERNATIVE

Comprehensive SEL programming is based on the understanding that the best learning emerges from supportive and challenging relationships and that many different kinds of problem behaviors are caused by the same risk factors. Developing and bolstering student strengths and preventing problems such as violence, drug abuse, or dropping out are most effective when multiyear, coordinated efforts develop children's social and emotional abilities through engaging classroom instruction, prosocial learning activities outside the classroom, and broad parent and community participation in program planning, implementation, and evaluation. Comprehensive programs begin at an early age and continue in a developmentally appropriate sequence through high school. In addition, recent research shows that systematically building students' key SEL skills results in increased academic success as well.

Uncoordinated programming assumes that the fix can and should be simple or quick. Such programming ignores the fact that problems such as poor achievement, youth drug use, violence, bullying, sexual promiscuity, and alienation are closely interrelated, complex, and develop over time within the broader context of the school, family, and community. When students fail or an unexpected outbreak of negative behavior among students occurs, the first question the public often asks is, "Who is to blame?" Typically, the next step is to adopt programs to "target" the problem or the offending children. Rarely, however, do the school, the parents, and the community come together to ask, "How can we provide a positive and supportive environment for our young people, from grades preK–12, which will be a lasting part of education in our community? How can we make events like these much less likely to occur in the future?"

What Exactly Is Social and Emotional Learning?

Daniel Goleman (1998) described the five basic categories of emotional and social skills or competencies that SEL programming works to impart:

- *Self-Awareness:* Knowing what we are feeling in the moment, and using those preferences to guide our decision making; having a realistic assessment of our own abilities and a well-grounded sense of self-confidence.
- *Self-Regulation:* Handling our emotions so that they facilitate rather than interfere with the task at hand; being conscientious and delaying gratification to pursue goals; recovering well from emotional distress.
- *Motivation:* Using our deepest preferences to move and guide us toward our goals, to help us take initiative and strive to improve, and to persevere in the face of setbacks and frustrations.
- *Empathy:* Sensing what people are feeling, being able to take their perspective, and cultivating rapport and attunement with a broad diversity of people.
- *Social Skills:* Handling emotions in relationships well and accurately reading social situations and networks; interacting smoothly; using these skills to persuade and lead, to negotiate and settle disputes, for cooperation and teamwork.

Research clearly demonstrates that these skills can be learned. SEL provides systematic classroom instruction that enhances children's capacities to recognize and manage their emotions, appreciate the perspectives of others, establish prosocial goals and solve problems, and use a variety of interpersonal skills to effectively and ethically handle developmentally relevant tasks. The result is greater success in school and life (cf. Hawkins, 1997; Zins et al., in press). SEL, then, is the process of teaching and developing these skills and competencies through classroom-based instruction, role-play, modeling, and reinforcement throughout the school day. Today there are numerous nationally available, evidence-based SEL programs, and in addition to social and emotional skills enhancement, many also include content focuses, including alcohol, tobacco, and other drug prevention; violence prevention; and sexuality, health, and character education. Some SEL programs also have specific components to foster safe, caring, and supportive learning environments in classrooms and throughout the school (in the lunchroom, on the playground, etc.). Such environments have been shown to build strong student attachment to school and motivation to learn—actions strongly associated with academic success. Another consequence is more collegial and respectful relationships among school staff members and a greater commitment to professionalism and excellence.

The SEL approach realistically addresses the needs of students at their psychosocial roots. Underachievement and harmful behaviors develop in part from a complex web of familial, economic, and cultural circumstances. These conditions are part of the fabric of life and are difficult to attack. Yet strategies that help children develop the resilience to cope adaptively with modern-day stresses can be effective, and it is there that schools need to focus their efforts.

Many educators want to provide systematic instruction that enhances SEL but don't know how to begin. Others are working to carry out SEL in limited ways but need clear information on the best evidence-based programs, how to implement them, how to combine them, and how to lead effectively the charge to sustain them, including generating stable sources of financial support. In 1994, an organization was formed to address these needs—the Collaborative for Academic, Social, and Emotional Learning (CASEL). The remainder of this chapter describes CASEL's work and the resources now available from CASEL to assist educational leaders.

SUPPORT FOR EDUCATORS WHO WANT TO IMPLEMENT SOCIAL AND EMOTIONAL LEARNING

In conducting research for his best-selling book *Emotional Intelligence: Why It Can Matter More Than IQ* (1995), *New York Times* science writer Daniel Goleman became aware of the fledgling SEL movement—a new and growing cross-disciplinary field that addressed the development of children's emotional awareness, their social problem-solving skills, and their avoidance of risky health behaviors. Goleman joined forces with a group of scientists, educators, and philanthropists to establish an organization that would be devoted to promoting SEL in all schools, from preschool through high school. Thus, CASEL was established. CASEL includes and collaborates with an international network of leading researchers and practitioners in the fields of SEL, prevention, positive youth development, service learning, character education, and education reform. Its mission is to foster children's success in school and life by establishing scientifically based SEL as an essential part of education from preschool through high school. To accomplish this mission, CASEL has been guided by six goals:

- Advance the science of SEL
- Translate scientific knowledge into effective school practices
- Promote SEL as a foundation for academic learning
- Disseminate information about evidence-based SEL educational strategies
- Enhance the professional preparation of educators so they have the tools to implement high-quality SEL instruction
- Network and collaborate with educators, scientists, policymakers, and interested citizens to promote and increase the coordination of SEL efforts

CASEL began by providing a conceptual and defining frame-work for the field of SEL with its 1997 book, *Promoting Social and Emotional Learning: Guidelines for Educators*, published by the Association for Supervision and Curriculum Development (ASCD) and distributed to more than 100,000 educators (Elias et al., 1997). CASEL also worked with ASCD to publish a special issue of *Educational Leadership* on SEL (ASCD, 1997). CASEL then turned to developing a strong base of scientific evidence of SEL impacts, with particular attention to social–emotional, academic, health, and behavioral outcomes. Numerous scholarly articles and books were produced (e.g., Weissberg & Greenberg, 1998; Zins, Elias, Greenberg, & Weissberg, 2000).

Building on this scientific foundation, CASEL then shifted its primary emphasis to advancing the practice of SEL. For example, one CASEL project developed preservice and inservice curricula for teachers. Another project was designed to support strong school–family partnerships (producing research-based strategies and materials that help educators enhance communication between families and schools and that promote parent involve-ment). Other projects focus on program implementation and eval-uation (identifying effective strategies for implementation, monitoring, and assessment of SEL practice). But the heart of CASEL's work is now focused on providing educational leaders—the key decision makers in schools and districts—with the tools they need to create effective SEL for their students.

Educational Leaders' Guidelines for Effective SEL Programming

CASEL developed a set of seven "Guidelines for Effective SEL Programming." Distilling research, experiential knowledge of educational leaders around the country about what makes for effective and sustained SEL programming, and federal and other national guidelines (e.g., Elias et al., 1997; Learning First Alliance, 2001; and the U.S. Department of Education's "Principles of Effectiveness"), CASEL articulated these seven guidelines that apply to any well-planned, effective SEL effort and are consistent as well with thinking about broader school reform. Effective schoolwide and districtwide SEL programming has the following characteristics:

1. *Effective SEL Is Grounded in Theory and Evidence.* Effective SEL programming uses approaches that are grounded in theory, so that implementers understand their key components in conceptual as well as operational terms. Effective SEL approaches also have strong empirical evidence of effectiveness based on scientific research.

2. *Effective SEL Is Developmentally and Socioculturally Appropriate Content.* Effective SEL programming is developmentally appropriate, with clearly specified learning objectives for each grade level. It starts before students are pressured to experiment with risky behaviors and continues through adolescence. It is also culturally appropriate, both in the sensitive and respectful manner in which it is implemented and in its content, which addresses cultural sensitivity, respect for others, and applications to culturally complex real-life situations.

3. *Effective SEL Promotes Skills and Core Ethical Values.* Effective SEL programming emphasizes students' cognitive, affective, and behavioral skills and their understanding of information about targeted social and health domains. It also addresses students' attitudes and values about themselves, others, and tasks, and their perceptions of social norms. It does so through both classroom lessons and practice throughout the school day. Too many ineffective programs stress knowledge about specific problems and fail to concentrate on the values and skills necessary to help children engage in positive academic and health behaviors.

4. *Effective SEL Coordinates Positive Youth Development and Problem Prevention Programming.* Effective SEL programming provides a coordinating framework for the otherwise fragmented array of efforts schools and districts undertake to promote the positive development of youth (e.g., through character education, service learning, mentoring, health promotion, etc.) and prevents problem behaviors (e.g., low achievement, substance abuse, bullying, pregnancy and AIDS prevention, delinquency, etc.). It is also critical to coordinate SEL with academic subjects addressed in the curriculum. Thus, SEL simultaneously—and seamlessly—addresses students' social, emotional, ethical, physical, and academic well-being, rather than focusing on one categorical outcome.

5. *Effective SEL Integrates Schoolwide, Family, and Community Partnerships.* Effective SEL programming is coordinated with all

academic instruction, as well as with mental health, health, and student support services. It also actively involves parents, community members, and school staff in ongoing application of SEL from the classroom to everyday life situations through modeling, feedback, and positive reinforcement.

6. *Effective SEL Addresses Critical Implementation Factors: Leadership, Resources, Policy Alignment, and Training.* Effective SEL programming addresses the factors that determine the long-term success or failure of school initiatives, including involved and supportive leaders who model SEL practices, adequate resources, and alignment with other policies that govern school practices. It also incorporates well-planned, high-quality training, professional development, technical support, and supervision.

7. *Effective SEL Includes Ongoing Evaluation and Continuous Improvement.* Effective SEL programming begins with needs assessment data to ensure appropriate fit between student needs and selected responses and then uses evaluative data for staff feedback and continuous improvement, to assess progress toward specified goals, and to provide accountability to stakeholders.

"Safe and Sound": The CASEL Review of SEL Programs

The guidelines provide educational leaders committed to SEL with a realistic picture of the scope of work involved, but the most pressing question often is, "Where do I start?" Once administrators are convinced of the need for SEL programming in their district, the best place to begin is with an evidence-based program that imparts SEL skills, effectively prevents problems, and helps students realize their best academic performance. To identify and share information about such programs, CASEL received funding from the Department of Education to prepare *Safe and Sound: An Educational Leaders' Guide to Evidence-Based Social and Emotional Learning Programs.* The guide is designed to help educators make wise choices among the large field of available programs and to help schools identify the strengths, weaknesses, and gaps in their current prevention efforts. Consistent with its commitment to promoting more comprehensive, coordinated efforts to prevent problem behaviors and build students' life skills, CASEL included in the SEL program review programs from a broad range of content areas. These include alcohol, tobacco, and other drug prevention; violence prevention; sexuality, health, and character education; and social skills enhancement. CASEL brought to each program the lens of SEL: The goal of the guide's ratings process is to determine the degree to which these programs incorporate key elements of a comprehensive, coordinated approach based on SEL.

As of this writing, the program review describes over 80 school-based prevention programs and provides ratings for these programs in 28 categories. These include 15 SEL competencies; coverage of six behavioral domains (substance abuse prevention, violence prevention, healthy sexual development, health promotion, promotion of citizenship, and promotion of academic achievement); coverage of schoolwide, family, and community coordination; and attention to program assessment and evaluation (Payton et al., 2000). In addition, CASEL collects information about the nature and extent of initial and ongoing training and technical assistance offered by the program purveyors as well as program cost information.

The guide also provides educational leaders with assistance in combining programs from different vendors to address the needs and behaviors of different grade levels and student groups; help in integrating these programs with existing student support services, counseling interventions, discipline policies, after-school programs, and other district efforts that address the social, emotional, and academic needs of students; and ideas for how to pay for these programs, both by accessing intermittent funds such as those made available from the multistate tobacco settlement, as well as with longer term and more stable funding mechanisms. (*Safe and Sound* is available at www.casel.org.)

EDUCATIONAL LEADERSHIP FOR THE 21ST CENTURY

Creating school- and districtwide comprehensive, coordinated SEL programming, in which schools and families work in partnership to promote knowledgeable, responsible, healthy, and caring children requires resourceful, emotionally intelligent leaders who have a vision of what they want to accomplish for 21st-century education. It also requires support from an organization committed to making this happen. CASEL is involved in a series of undertakings that will help educational leaders use SEL programming to its greatest effectiveness in improving student well-being and school success. In addition to the creation of tools to guide program content, selection, and implementation, CASEL has identified districts that have put comprehensive SEL programming into place. These serve as case studies and demonstration sites from which others can learn what they might create in their own districts (in Immanuel Kant's famous dictum, "the actual proves the possible").

CASEL is also expanding its work with educational leaders to create a network of national and regional organizations to advance SEL science, policy, and practice. This involves establishing professional associations among SEL leaders, distributing newsletters, offering opportunities to network and attend informational sessions at major professional meetings, developing specialized training institutes, and working to create policy supports, including noncategorical funding streams, at the state and federal levels.

To provide children with the best possible education in these challenging times, we need a new approach that understands that the best we can do for children—academically, socially, and emotionally—is support their full growth and development. SEL is an integrative framework that gives schools the means to do exactly that. As the CASEL guidelines and projects suggest, the future of SEL in the schools is both complicated and promising. It requires strong, informed, and visionary leadership. CASEL is committed to working in partnership with educators and leading educational organizations to support educational leaders in this work, believing that when development, achievement, and prevention are conceived in the best interests of children, we will have education in the fullest sense of the word.

REFERENCES

Association for Supervision and Curriculum Development. (1997, May). Social and emotional learning. *Educational Leadership, 54*(8), Alexandria, VA: Association for Supervision and Curriculum Development.

Elias, M. J., Zins, J. E., Weissberg, R. P., Frey, K. S., Greenberg, M. T., Haynes, N. M., Kessler, R., Schwab-Stone, M. E., & Shriver, T. P. (1997). *Promoting social and emotional learning: Guidelines for educators.* Alexandria, VA: Association for Supervision and Curriculum Development.

Goleman, D. (1995). *Emotional intelligence: Why it can matter more than IQ.* New York: Bantam.

Goleman, D. (1998). *Working with emotional intelligence.* New York: Bantam.

Hawkins, J. D. (1997). Academic performance and school success: Sources and consequences. In R. P. Weissberg, T. P. Gullotta, R. L. Hampton, B. A. Ryan, & G. R. Adams (Eds.), *Enhancing children's wellness* (pp. 278–305). Thousand Oaks, CA: Sage.

Learning First Alliance. (2001). *Every child learning: Safe and supportive schools.* Washington, DC: Author.

Payton, J. W., Graczyk, P. A., Wardlaw, D. M., Bloodworth, M., Tompsett, C. J., & Weissberg, R. P. (2000). Social and emotional learning: A framework for promoting mental health and reducing risk behavior in children and youth. *Journal of School Health, 70,* 179–185.

Shriver, T. P., & Weissberg, R. P. (1996, May 15) No new wars! *Education Week, XV,* 33, 37.

Weissberg, R. P., & Greenberg, M. T. (1998). School and community competence-enhancement and prevention programs. In W. Damon (Series Ed.); I. E. Sigel & K. A. Renninger (Vol. Eds.), *Handbook of child psychology: Vol. 4. Child psychology in practice* (5th ed., pp. 877–954). New York: John Wiley.

Zins, J. E., Elias, M. J., Greenberg, M. T., & Weissberg, R. P. (2000). Promoting social and emotional competence in children. In K. M. Minke & G. C. Bear (Eds.), *Preventing school problems—promoting school success: Strategies and programs that work* (pp. 71–99). Washington, DC: National Association of School Psychologists.

Zins, J. E., Weissberg, R. P. Wang, M. C., & Walberg, H. J. (Eds.). (In press). *Social and emotional learning and school success.* New York: Teachers College Press.

CHAPTER THREE

Social–Emotional Learning and Academic Achievement

Marcia Knoll

Janet Patti

By its very nature, being socially and emotionally intelligent contributes to academic achievement.

This statement is of profound importance to those concerned with the future of education. In this chapter, we discuss and explore the statement by comparing five aspects of the teaching and learning process with the attributes of social–emotional literacy. First, we discuss *readiness to learn* by presenting how the social and emotional skills that an individual learner brings to a learning environment contribute to learning that is maximally effective. Second, we consider the *climate of the classroom* and how it contributes to achievement. Third, we present examples of *instructional strategies* that use social and emotional competencies as contributors to learning. Fourth, we provide examples of how the *content of the curriculum* can be better understood and remembered when it is taught through the lens of social–emotional competencies. Last, we consider how social and emotional competency affect students' abilities to prepare for, take, and ultimately achieve on *assessment tests*.

READINESS TO LEARN REQUIRES SOCIAL–EMOTIONAL COMPETENCE

Consider for a moment 10-year-old Mario's development of social and emotional competency in the area of "self and others." Can Mario identify his own feelings? Can he understand and manage them in an emotionally charged situation such as an argument or when he strikes out in a baseball game? Can he remain calm rather than act out in class even when he feels frustrated during a literacy lesson? When he comes to class in the morning after a night in which his parents were arguing incessantly and not subject his hurt and angry feelings on his classmates or his teacher?

What about 10-year-old David? Can he recognize that he has a learning disability that impacts his ability to learn mathematics? Can he understand that he will become frustrated from time to time and unable to keep up with other children in his class? Will he be willing to ask a neighbor to help him or be willing raise his hand so that the teacher can explain the problem to him? Will he try to hide his disability from his friends, or accept it as a limitation with which he must work that doesn't make him inferior to other students? Finally, can Mario and David's teacher recognize the individual challenges that both boys confront and incorporate that knowledge into ways to help them in the teaching and learning process?

The attributes of social–emotional literacy clearly define the learner's readiness to learn and the ability of the environment to meet the learner at least half way. An awareness of self and others is among the most basic of these attributes. Being aware of one's own feelings and understanding that everyone has feelings allows young people to work on social and emotional competencies in the same way that children would work to improve other classroom skills. For example, if 6-year-old Martha is feeling sad because her best friend has moved away, she might be able to talk about this with her teacher, or class-mates. By simply recognizing and expressing her emotions, chances are that her sadness will not interfere with her learning process. Furthermore, if we teach youngsters how to recognize their strengths and weaknesses, they can begin to understand how to use their strengths to overcome their weaknesses and become more confident and optimistic learners. The mistake too often made by well-meaning educators is to attempt to separate the child's readiness ability from the learning process, thereby eliminating the social and emotional development of the child from the daily workings of the classroom. Subsequently, the child finds it difficult to acquire the new skills that will enhance learning. Bruce Perry, professor of child psychiatry in Texas and expert on the neurobiology of child trauma, reminds us of the following:

> Genetics and experience work together in ways that give us each a set of individual preferences and personalities. Some children are timid, some bold. Some like to observe, some are more active. Some children like dinosaurs, some like dolls. With optimal experiences, the brain develops healthy, flexible and diverse capabilities. When there is a disruption of the timing, intensity, quality or quantity of normal developmental experiences however, there may be a devastating impact on neurodevelopment. (Perry, n.d.)

Sad though it may be, children today are struggling mightily to balance their home and community lives with that of their classroom life. The social ills that our children confront, such as divorce, abuse, domestic violence, poverty, bullying, and social injustice, clearly find their way through the classroom doors. As a result, social interaction skills are vital to every student's success in school. The nature of their interactions enhances or inhibits learning. Schools are social institutions bringing large numbers of children and adults together for many hours of the day. Some parents teach their children, from an early age, how to share resources, to get along with others, and to wait their turn, thus preparing them for the social interactions they will encounter in school. The first year of organized school, as well as subsequent years, may be difficult for those students who have not learned these skills. The "habits of mind" of young people and their readiness to learn can be strongly shaped by increasing their social–emotional skill level.

Indeed, the world of knowledge opens up to learners who can listen to the perspectives of others. Additional ideas from many points of view contribute to a fuller understanding of the topic. These learners understand that the first answer is not the only answer. These attributes make the student better able to deal with the challenges and opportunities of the classroom and less likely to explode when someone does not agree with his or her idea. As Dr. Perry noted, "What we are as adults is the product of the world we experienced as children. The way a society functions is a reflection of the child rearing practices of that society" (Perry, n.d.). Young people who can consider a variety of perspectives and formulate their own opinions about issues and events are ready to face the complex challenges of a diverse world. Certainly, the events of September 11, 2001, should bring home to every serious educational leader the importance of these skills.

Communication is a key aspect of readiness to learn. Students who know how to express themselves clearly and appropriately both verbally and nonverbally are better able to make their thoughts and feelings known to the teacher and to their peers. Being a good listener is a critical part of this process; students who listen actively to others demonstrate that the message sent has been understood. Conflicts caused by miscommunications are reduced.

Finally, a cornerstone social–emotional attribute, the set of skills needed for being a responsible decision maker, makes the student ready to learn. The classroom is filled with situations that require students to make decisions about how to act, behave, and respond. Students who are socially and emotionally competent and ready to learn have the capacity to identify those situations that require them to make a decision and how to choose among academic and social considerations. They evaluate situations and assess their best course of action or inaction based on the risks involved, barriers to their success, and available resources.

As we think about providing children and young adults with the education they need to be successful in life, we must widen our view beyond teaching them how to achieve at high levels on statewide tests. The young person who has mastered social and emotional competence will be able to access the many choices and opportunities that life provides and put their acquired knowledge to productive use in society.

CLASSROOM CLIMATES MUST ESTABLISH A TONE OF INTELLECTUAL AND PERSONAL INTEGRITY

Among the most important of teachers' roles is to create and maintain a healthy, productive, social–emotional climate in the classroom. In so doing, teachers demonstrate through their communications and actions that they are confident and enthusiastic about making the classroom a safe place for successful learners. They greet their students with a smile when they enter the classroom and engage them in conversations. They express interest in each student as an individual and as a member of the class. Their facial expression and body language are accepting of student needs, and their speaking voice is clear, easy to hear, and easy to understand. The teacher's physical vitality demonstrates involvement, energy, and interest in the teaching role.

With their students, teachers establish a code of behavior that everyone will follow. This code of behavior emphasizes mutual respect, appreciation, and acceptance of others. Hurtful behaviors such as name-calling, blaming, and ridiculing are not permitted because they prevent the student from learning and may impede the learning process for others who fear that they will be next.

The attitude projected in a positive learning environment makes vividly apparent the students' readiness to learn. They are encouraged to take personal responsibility by engaging in safe and healthy behaviors. All participants in the learning environment believe in themselves and in their ability to learn. By being fair and honest with themselves and with others, the need for name-calling and blame is reduced. Students in this kind of classroom environment give themselves the opportunity to ask for help. They realize that everyone in their learning environment is a resource. Rather than punching and playing tricks, they demonstrate this belief through their respect, appreciation, and acceptance of individuals and groups who may sound or look different from them.

In these classrooms, teachers have high expectations. They expect their students to learn and achieve, and they believe that success is possible for all students; it is their job to find a way to make that happen. They believe that problems can be resolved rather than simply endured. They seek solutions to problems they cannot solve by speaking with members of the educational community. Teachers try to continuously strive for new ways to help students to achieve. These actions send messages to the students that their teacher is there to help them in whatever ways are required to help them succeed. The young people are empowered to become part of the solution rather than the problem.

The climate of social and emotional classrooms in which students achieve is work oriented. A tone of intellectual and personal integrity is established. The teacher focuses on learning and communicates in words and actions what is expected in terms of student behavior, attitude, and work. In these classrooms, teachers develop and discuss with the class lists or rubrics that specify the ways students can demonstrate their positive behavior and the high level of work that is expected from them. This list is then posted or distributed to everyone in the learning environment. Students use these lists or rubrics by themselves or with others to compare their actions and work with what is expected.

Class meetings are a regular ritual in the social–emotional learning (SEL) classroom. Students know that their voices will be heard, that there is time set aside each week to discuss classroom problems. Young people know that their opinion matters and will be considered. In this classroom climate, young people choose to resolve conflict nonviolently and possess the skills to do so. "Peace corners" are commonly found in the classroom so that students can reflect on actions taken or to be considered. Mediators are present. Social and emotional support is an expected norm of this classroom.

The teacher who understands the importance of a warm and supportive environment uses praise so that it is helpful and encouraging rather than harmful and discouraging. These teachers do not praise unimportant or trivial tasks. Praise for an easy task or praise for actions that are below the student's ability send the message that the student lacks the ability to do more or better work and that the teacher has low expectations for the student's success. Teachers know that praise is appreciated, believed, and accepted when it is reserved for something important. Unearned or empty praise is replaced with acknowledgment and suggestions, for example, "You were able to complete some of the math problems correctly, but there are others that you still need to work on." These teachers also know that true praise is specific rather than general. Instead of repeatedly saying, "Good job," they specify precisely what was good about the job, for example, "You identified some excellent resources for your group to use."

Students' contributions are treated with respect. Student work decorates the walls of the classroom and the halls of the school. Students in these classrooms have learned about respect, and they model the respect and caring demonstrated by their teachers. They treat the teacher, other students, and their work in these same ways. The challenge to the teacher of this classroom, however, is to meet all students at their current point along the SEL continuum to help them acquire the skills to enhance academic competency. Therefore, the teacher must be well versed in diverse instructional strategies that can be incorporated into lessons to enhance each student's learning.

THE PEDAGOGY OF SEL CREATES CRITICAL THINKING, COOPERATION, AND CREATIVITY

Much has been learned about the teaching and learning process since the days when many of us grew up in classes with straight rows, student silence, and the teacher lecturing at the front of the room. Active learning promotes retention. In fact, the most assured method of retaining information involves students' constructing for themselves a sense of meaning from the newly learned material and then teaching it to others. An emotional connection to the learning increases the chances that all students—all learners—will retain what they learn. With the teacher's guidance, today's children take responsibility for facilitating their own learning and encouraging the learning of their classmates. Teachers in effective classrooms use a variety of affectively oriented instructional strategies that involve the learner and promote the development and use of the learner's SEL competencies. We outline these strategies next.

Cooperative Learning

Cooperative learning strategies are excellent vehicles for this form of instruction. In cooperative groups, children regulate their feelings. They work productively with others to complete specific tasks. They listen to the perspectives of everyone in the group. They recognize the importance of being trustworthy, dependable, and accountable for their contribution to the required work. Young people are challenged to openly communicate their thoughts and feelings and actively listen to others. They jointly make decisions that contribute to the success or failure of the group. To do this, they brainstorm ideas, generate alternatives, and choose the best solution. When problems arise, they assume responsibility for resolving them in creative, peaceful ways. The extent of learning that occurs for young people who learn to work cooperatively is enormous. Educational leaders who promote the use of these instructional strategies recognize that 21st-century learning must have multiple objectives for their students. Although the content of the learning is essential, so, too, are the social and emotional competencies and intellectual habits being practiced and learned.

Journal Writing

Journal writing is a wonderful way to help students improve their writing skills as they develop their social and emotional competencies. Students are able to express their feelings openly. If they are troubled about personal issues, they can write about them. Anger, frustration, fear, disappointment, and unhappiness have their place in the journal with responsibility, joy, happiness, and success. Students can also be challenged by using their journal to reflect on specific SEL competencies. If Mario had been asked to express in writing his feelings about his parents' constant arguing, he would have had the opportunity to release the pent up emotion that he brought into the classroom that morning. He might have then chosen to share the feelings expressed in his writing with one other student in a pair-shared activity that could have followed this writing activity. Teachers could also follow up journal activity by asking students to place concerns they might have in a special box so that if Mario feels he might like to talk about his concerns with a counselor, his teacher could arrange this.

Journal writing is also a good method to help young people practice ways to think critically and make responsible decisions. They could be asked to explore in writing a variety of options to solving a given problem that has arisen in the class or that was derived from a fictional character in a literature selection or from history or current events.

Debates and Dialogues

In a related way, dialogues and debates provide excellent opportunities for combining SEL competencies with critical thinking and creativity in subject areas. These require preestablished behavior norms so that young people feel safe to express their feelings without rejection and to process these feelings creatively with others. The debate process teaches respect for the rights of all people to think and believe as they wish. All classroom participants appreciate different points of view, although not everyone necessarily agrees with them. Accurately understanding different perspectives enables students to present a strong position for their point of view. This helps young people acquire the language of assertion and creative argumentation, which may help them stand up for themselves in difficult situations, such as being bullied or belittled by someone else or championing a difficult cause. Conflict resolution skills such as negotiation may come in handy when trying to reach a decision that satisfies everyone involved.

Script Writing and Role-Playing

Script writing and role-playing are excellent vehicles for learning and using social and emotional competencies while enhancing language arts skills. Writing a believable script entails seeing a situation from the perspective of each of the characters. Individual differences among the characters in the script make them real. What characters do rather than who they are is what makes the reader accept or reject them as individuals. As students identify the central problem in the script, they must reflect on and examine possible risks, barriers, and resources and develop strategies for resolving these difficulties. Teachable moments about life's dilemmas find their ways through many language arts and literature lessons.

Role-playing provides different opportunities to learn and use social and emotional competencies during speech development. But for this strategy to be successful, students must be aware of the feelings and perspectives of the characters they portray. In the process of uncovering the feelings of the character, the students compare and understand their own feelings. In a role-play situation, students have a perfect opportunity to experience how to be aware of and manage their own feelings. Debriefing these experiences with the class also helps students explore and use these competencies.

Technology

Technology is yet another classroom tool that children and young adults can use to increase both their subject content knowledge and their social and emotional competencies. After students do some individual research on a topic, they can come together to share their research and plan a final presentation that can be made in a variety of media and formats. In this process, students can explore the variety of points of view represented in the class. They use SEL skills to explore these points of view and reach consensus about what to include in the final presentation and how to present it. Technology becomes a tool the group uses to create a document that presents an agreed-upon perspective.

IMPLEMENTING SOCIAL AND EMOTIONAL LEARNING THROUGH SUBJECT CONTENT

Almost every content area provides opportunities to promote the development of social and emotional competencies. As teachers consider the content of particular courses, they may find many opportunities to enhance achievement through learning and practicing social and emotional competency. Some examples are presented in the following sections.

Language Arts

Increase students' respect for others by focusing reading assignments on the variety of cultures represented at the school. Reading about and then reporting on a culture different from one's own helps students accept and appreciate individual and group differences. Conflicts caused by a misunderstanding of these differences can be eliminated.

Students can become adept at problem identification and solution by examining the problems faced by characters in a book and evaluating the solution that was selected. They can express their points of view and offer other solutions in an essay. The competency of social responsibility can be developed by reading the newspaper to identify current community issues. Students can be asked to write a letter to the appropriate agency stating their points of view about an issue.

Science

Environmental studies provide many opportunities to teach and learn social responsibility. Students can explore their own community as well as the global community and explore ways to protect the environment. Using scientific data can develop problem-solving competencies. Students can learn how to develop, implement, and evaluate positive and informed solutions to problems based on data they have collected on the subject. Similarly, using collected data, such as data acquired by conducting a survey to make a decision about the lunch schedule, helps students learn decision-making skills.

Social Studies

Students can develop and refine their negotiation skills by exploring conflicts in history. Give the students the opportunity to negotiate and peacefully resolve a particular historical conflict to the satisfaction of all involved. For example, students might try their hand at negotiating the conflict that preceded the Revolutionary War, the War of 1812, or the Opium Wars. Students might enjoy finding their own solution to the problems created by the various forms of currency in the colonies at the time the Articles of Confederation were created.

Perspective taking is an interesting way to view history and to learn social and emotional competency. History is filled with incidents of prejudice and discrimination. While learning this, students may develop the social and emotional competency to value the rights of all peoples. A study of Native Americans, Black Americans, Japanese Americans during World War II, or the peoples of the Middle East in the late 20th and early 21st centuries may help students appreciate the importance of accurately understanding the perspectives of others and of developing the critical thinking and SEL tools needed to do so.

Health Education

The health curriculum is a natural place to develop social and emotional competencies that lead to success in school and life. Being personally responsible means engaging in safe and healthy behaviors. These behaviors are taught in the health curriculum, but engaging students in activities that use the pedagogy of SEL to simulate the real world and the emotionality and interpersonal conflict that surrounds many health decisions may make students carry their learning outside of the classroom. Students who recognize their strengths and weaknesses have a constructive sense of self that helps them handle everyday challenges with self-confidence and optimism, rather than in the form of substance abuse or other unsafe behavior.

ASSESSMENT OUTCOMES ARE LINKED TO SOCIAL–EMOTIONAL COMPETENCIES

As the test taking reform movement continues to sweep through our nation's schools, young people are faced with the challenge of passing state-mandated tests. Some students are better test takers than others; their learning styles align well with the mathematical and linguistic challenges that these tests pose. Other students may have strengths in other intelligences, such as spatial ability that can be demonstrated in art projects or physical puzzles and technical projects. Still others are more auditory and respond better to musical challenges and the sounds and symbols of other languages. For many students, taking a performance assessment is a far better way to determine what they actually know, than is responding to short-answer questions and writing essays.

Today and in the foreseeable future, high-stakes testing is and will be a way of life in almost every state. Educational leaders must prepare students for the challenges that these tests present. One responsibility of educational leaders is to recognize and act on well-established information regarding test outcomes: Performing successfully on an examination requires much more than knowing the information. It requires knowing both how to prepare and how to take the assessment. In short, being a successful test taker requires social and emotional competencies.

Test anxiety and other problems contribute to student failure. Some students arrive at school on the day of the test with the stresses of family and deep-seated concerns about loved ones who may be absent, sick, or even dying. For other students, it is a history of poor performance on tests that keeps them from coming to the test in a relaxed state. Stress-reducing techniques such as talking about and facing fears, asking for help, and learning how to breathe from the diaphragm can help many students control their anxiety so that they can perform closer to their capacities.

Being a successful test taker begins with an awareness of oneself and with the concept of preparation. Students who are successful on assessments are aware of their feelings. They recognize their fear and apprehension about performance, but they are able to regulate those feelings by talking with someone supportive or by writing in a journal to use their fears as motivation to succeed. These students set positive and realistic goals that they are able to achieve, such as setting aside a quiet place and specific periods of time for study, and they work toward these goals. They can identify what is in their own best interest, and they delay entertainment and individual forms of enjoyment so that they can work persistently to prepare for the assessment. Students who are successful on assessments can identify the need for support and assistance and seek ways to get what they need. They may involve peers in study groups or trusted adults. They openly seek assistance and explore many resources to satisfy their need for help.

Of course, these are learned skills, and so children whose home environments are able to support and shape these patterns early and consistently are at a distinct advantage during the assessment process. In this way, assessment results are reflective of a student's life history, intertwined with his or her content knowledge.

CLOSING THOUGHTS

Academic achievement and social–emotional competencies are interwoven. Together they form the fabric of school success for each student by supporting learning for individuals and the group, by building shared responsibility and interdependence, by contributing to knowledge acquisition and retention, and by providing an inclusive learning environment that enhances achievement. In the 21st century, academic achievement and social–emotional competencies appear to be essential ingredients for a happy and successful life. Serious educational leaders with integrity have little choice but to meet the challenge of preparing students with the skills they need for success in both of these domains. Fortunately, they will find themselves with effective support as they join the growing ranks of excited and rejuvenated colleagues who have begun to embark on this path.

REFERENCES

Perry, B. D. (n.d.). *A place for everyone: Nurturing each child's niche* (Scholastic Teacher Resource Center). Retrieved from teacher. scholastic.com/professional/bruceperry/niche.htm.

CHAPTER FOUR

Lessons for Life

How Smart Schools Boost Academic, Social, and Emotional Intelligence

Alan M. Blankstein

While psychologist Abraham Maslow was developing his hierarchy of human needs, he spent some time with the Blackfoot Indians to gain insight into their child-rearing practices. He once recounted being in a room of elders and becoming aware of a little boy pushing on the heavy door to gain entrance into the room where they were all seated. At first, Maslow wondered why none of the elders simply opened the door for the child. After several minutes passed in which the child repeatedly pushed on the door to no avail, Maslow recalled thinking that these Blackfoot were indeed a cruel and callous lot.

Finally, after trying for perhaps 10 minutes, the child reared back, threw his whole body into the door and came tumbling inside the room as the door gave way. The elders stood and cheered for the boy and his success. It was at that moment that Maslow understood how truly caring these people were to have had the patience to allow that child to learn such an important lesson and to experience success, accomplishment, and self-control.

Characteristics such as self-awareness, problem-solving abilities, good communication skills, and a positive sense of self were once systematically developed in young people by many indigenous groups, including the Blackfoot Indians. But whose job is it to develop such vital skills in our children today? Although many would say, "It's the parents' job," the realities, for many reasons, often contradict this assumption.

"This class sucks!" "Leave me the ---- alone!" "I don't want to do this and you can't make me!"

These and even more antisocial statements and behaviors are common in today's classrooms. Teachers must deal with these kinds of comments and aggressive behaviors when they arise, but it is rarely part of their training. Even less common are systematic, schoolwide approaches or sets of tools to develop social and emotional skills in students. Many educators, especially at the high school level, would argue that this is not even their job.

In fact, as James Comer and Tim Shriver have indicated, teaching social and emotional skills always has been a part of the schooling experience (HOPE Foundation, 1999). The challenges now are the following:

1. How do we teach social and emotional skills to a classroom of children whose home experiences range from having had a great deal of preparation in this area to having had none at all?

2. How exactly do we teach these skills? What tools are available for this?

3. How can we take time for even one more thing in our already crowded curriculum?

A TOOL FOR HELPING TEACHERS BUILD STUDENTS' EQ SKILLS

Drawing on the Lessons for Life program, this article provides both a framework and specific strategies to help answer these questions. The benefits of using a comprehensive social–emotional learning

(SEL) approach such as Lessons for Life are seen in students' academic and career success (Gardner, 1983; Goleman, 1995) and in changes in the school community. Staff and students alike come to have a stake in the school climate and are motivated to make it better (Dasho, Lewis, Watson, & Schaps, in press).

There is currently a daunting number of SEL programs available to educators—more than 300 as of this writing. Educators can hardly deal knowledgeably with this kind of diversity. To arrive at a set of core principles, my colleagues and I at the National Center for Innovation and Education called on leaders in the SEL field to help reach a consensus. We involved individuals from many top programs, leaders from the Collaborative for Academic, Social, and Emotional Learning (CASEL), and educators from some of the most effective "SEL-friendly" schools in North America. We analyzed the principles that embodied what was working most consistently for school staff and students. These principles were then translated into the REGS (Relationships, Emotions, Goal Setting) model:

1. Caring relationships form the foundation for learning.

2. Emotions affect how and what we learn—including academic learning.

3. Goal setting and problem solving provide direction and energy for learning.

Let's consider how Principles 1 and 2 can play out in reality.

CARING RELATIONSHIPS FORM THE FOUNDATION FOR LEARNING

Increasingly, students are coming to school in an emotional state that is not conducive to learning. When students come to school upset, those feelings often need to be dealt with before any academic progress can be made. Take the following scenario, for example:

James's mother and father had a big fight in the morning before he went to school. His father hit his mother, and James ran out of the house to escape the scene. Realizing the school bus was going to come shortly, James went directly to the bus stop without getting his books from home. His initial fear and anger was compounded by the fact that he was going to arrive at school unprepared. James entered school feeling very angry, and ready to "go off." He wore his hat into class as a means of expressing his anger and engaging his teacher.

Teacher: James, take that hat off! You know we don't allow hats in class.

James: What hat?

Teacher: James, don't play games with me. Take it off, or you'll have to leave.

James: To hell with this stupid class—I'm out of here!

This kind of exchange is common in schools across the country, and teachers are challenged to recognize, quickly analyze, and effectively respond to the emotional issues students bring with them to school. There is no substitute for having a good, caring relationship with students (Principle 1 in Lessons for Life), and had one been in place, this situation may not have played out in the same manner. For example, Lessons for Life demonstrates that greeting students at the classroom door provides both a warm welcome for them and a chance to detect and quickly defuse any issues they may be bringing with them from outside. This one strategy alone may have enabled the teacher to pull James aside to address the situation quickly and privately before he entered the classroom.

Having a positive relationship with James may have also provided this teacher with alternatives to a head-on confrontation. The teacher may instead have used humor ("Well that hat *does* look good on you, but I will not be able to take my eyes off of it for the whole class and I won't be able to teach! How about if you show it to me after the bell rings, OK?") or a private moment with the student next to his desk while class was in progress ("James, I'm concerned about you because you're a smart guy and know that wearing your hat is against the rules. Could we talk a minute after class about how you're doing? In the meantime, would you take your hat off for me?").

The relationship provides a gateway for learning; it opens up opportunities to reach James. Ultimately, however, he will need to learn to understand and manage his emotions.

TAPPING EMOTIONS TO ENHANCE STUDENT LEARNING

First, let's examine how negative emotions can impede learning. Imagine that you have a serious argument with your spouse before leaving for work. If you are like many people, your ability to concentrate on work may be "crowded out" to some extent, because thoughts and feelings about the incident and what will happen as a result enter into what is known as your "working memory." As a result, receiving any kind of professional development immediately following the incident would be less effective than at another time, when emotions of anger, fear, or worry were not present. Similarly, James was in no condition to learn. Had he not provoked the confrontation, he still would likely not have absorbed much during that class period.

In Lessons for Life, we provide the following four-step process for helping young people understand and manage their emotions:

- *Identify and acknowledge your feelings.* What are the physical signs—sweaty palms, clenched jaw, lower back pain, stomachache—that indicate you are feeling upset? What are the emotional signs? The object is to help young people quickly identify and then be able to articulate how they are feeling. Acknowledging there is a problem is the first step to resolving it.
- *Determine your emotional triggers.* For some students, mentioning something about their mother will set off a reaction of rage. For others, it may be calling them "stupid." Whatever the case, "forewarned is forearmed," and our role is to help students prepare for and channel their emotional reactions.
- *Stay calm.* Techniques for helping students stay calm and have self-control include using peaceful imagery and deep breathing.
- *Reflect.* Role-playing situations and discussing them afterward, debriefing after an emotional outburst, and teaching children self-talk are among the techniques that will enable them to learn from each situation so that they can improve their capacity to manage their emotions.

Emotions can also be tapped to enhance learning. In Piscataway, New Jersey, for example, schools integrate emotions into the curriculum by asking students in social studies class to imagine themselves as part of the culture they are studying. The students are then asked to deduce the reasons for various behaviors of that culture based on how they would feel and respond in that time and setting.

The Responsive Classroom, as used in a Washington, DC, elementary school, involves beginning each day with warm-up exercises that ensure each student feels connected to the others and to the teacher. In so doing, they create a climate in which learning is associated with positive feelings, thus increasing motivation to learn while actually enhancing students' memory.

By consciously providing students with social and emotional learning opportunities using the REGS model in ways like those described here, teachers can actually gain instructional time that would otherwise be spent "putting out fires." Moreover, including an SEL component in the curriculum will not only enhance students' behavior, but their academic success as well (see Chapters 2 and 3 of this volume).

Lessons for Life, based in large part on the Association for Supervision and Curriculum Development's *Promoting Social and Emotional Learning: Guidelines for Educators* (Elias et al., 1997), includes three videos with specific examples and a detailed Leader's Guide to provide the tools needed for inservice and pre-service SEL education for teachers. It represents a way to respond to the crises and challenges in our schools by providing ways for both new and veteran teachers to bring SEL into their classroom, into their interactions with students, and into the school as a whole. James Comer anchors each video, which feature members of CASEL and CASEL-affiliated educators and consultation schools. In sum, Lessons for Life is a statement that violence, fear, neglect, and other strong negative emotions are the greatest enemies to genuine, lasting learning and that educators do not have to throw up their hands in frustration because they were not adequately trained to deal with these issues. Not only can we reclaim our at-risk youth, we can also strengthen all students. This clearly seems worth the continued efforts that are required.

REFERENCES

Dasho, S., Lewis, C., Watson, M., & Schaps, E. (In press). Fostering emotional intelligence in the classroom and school: Strategies from the Child Development Project. In J. Cohen (Ed.), *Social emotional learning and the young child: The foundation for academic and character development.* New York: Teachers College Press.

Elias, M., Zins, J., Weissberg, R., Frey, K., Greeberg, M., Haynes, N., Kessler, R., Schwab-Stone, M., Shriver, T. (1997). *Promoting social and emotional learning: Guidelines for educators.* Alexandria, VA: Association for Supervision and Curriculum Development.

Gardner, H. (1983). *Frames of mind: The theory of multiple intelligences.* New York: Basic Books.

Goleman, D. (1995). *Emotional intelligence: Why it can matter more than IQ.* New York: Bantam.

HOPE Foundation. (1999). *Lessons for life: How smart schools boost academic, social, and emotional intelligence.* Bloomington, IN: Author.

CHAPTER FIVE

How New Knowledge About the Brain Applies to Social and Emotional Learning

Ronald S. Brandt

What is "brain-compatible" teaching, and how does it apply to social and emotional learning? With findings about the brain being publicized at conferences and in the mass media, educators naturally want to know how they can apply this new knowledge as they struggle to bring a generation of young people to higher standards. Because of my long interest in learning, and because I have participated in several invitational meetings at which educators and neuroscientists discussed the use of brain research in schools, I address this timely, fascinating question here, even though the answer is not completely clear.

Before considering how brain-based education applies to social and emotional learning, I had better start with the broader question of what educational practices, if any, can be justified by what is known about the brain. Below briefly, are capsule views of consultants who specialize in interpreting brain science to educators.

WHAT CONSULTANTS SAY ABOUT THE APPLICATION OF BRAIN RESEARCH

David Sousa (1998) argued that "what we are discovering about learning from brain research has the potential for making the greatest contribution to our practice in recent memory" (p. 52). Referring to new findings about memory, emotion, and sensory engagement, he advised that "Classrooms should be busy, interactive environments. . . . At appropriate intervals, students should be standing up, moving around, and discussing with each other what they are learning *while* they are learning it" (p. 35).

Renate Nummela Caine and Geoffrey Caine (1997, p. 19) listed 12 interrelated learning principles (such as "The search for meaning is innate" and "Learning always involves conscious and unconscious processes"), which they formulated from a wide range of sources, especially brain research. Based on these principles, they advised that educational experiences should have three qualities: relaxed alertness, orchestrated immersion in complex experience, and active processing. The richness of their ideas cannot be conveyed in a few words, but in general, the style of education they advocate is substantially different from conventional practice. Brain-based teaching is "more learner centered because genuine student interest is at its core . . . with experiences that approach the complexity of real life" (p. 219).

Another popular consultant, Susan Kovalik (1994), developed a complete model of teaching, called Integrated Thematic Instruction (ITI). The curriculum in an ITI classroom is organized around a yearlong theme that incorporates key concepts. As much as possible, meaningful content is learned in real-life situations. Students are provided many choices. As they work on teacher-planned "inquiries," they are encouraged to practice life skills, such as integrity, curiosity, and responsibility.

Eric Jensen, who has written several books about the brain, made numerous practical suggestions for *Teaching With the Brain in Mind* (1998). Like Kovalik, he recommended that students be given choices and that curriculum content be engaging and relevant ("make it personal: relate to family, neighborhood, city, life stages, love, health, and so on," p. 48). He advocated physical movement, music, and extensive use of color, emphasizing the importance of emotions in learning.

Based on her study of brain research, Pat Wolfe (1997) called for an enriched learning environment. She defined this as "stimulating and challenging, and in which the students' minds are actively involved" (pp. 23–24). She noted that projects are "a rich source of both learning and motivation" (pp. 31–32) and recommended simulation, role-playing, and learning through direct experience.

Biologist Robert Sylwester (1995) seldom prescribes classroom practice on the basis of the brain science he explains. "Current brain theory and research now provide only the broad tantalizing outlines of what the school of the future might be," he wrote (p. 41). But he has offered hints about the kinds of school programs he considers appropriate when he advocates "thematic curricula" and advised taking advantage of "our brain's strengths" (such "cooperating and conceptualizing," rather than "things that require solitary sustained attention and precision," p. 141). He also described the ideal teaching environment as "continually changing and challenging" and teachers as "facilitators who help to shape a stimulating social environment" (p. 139).

AN APPARENT CONSENSUS EXISTS . . . OR DOES IT?

These well-informed consultants have different backgrounds and points of view, but they appear to have quite similar conceptions of desirable educational practice. They say brain research shows that curriculum content should be interesting and relevant and that students should learn cooperatively through active engagement in realistic activities. These recommendations are generally consistent with a style of schooling characterized for years as progressive, as opposed to traditionalist.

Some observers might describe their conclusions not as objective science but as a continuation of a long-standing commitment of leaders of American education to a romantic vision of schooling (Ravitch, 1983). They might even suggest that, as members of a single-minded professional community, the consultants were already committed to the progressive philosophy before they encountered brain research, and so found what they were looking for.

I know each of these consultants personally, and I respect their intellectual honesty. But as an educator long committed to innovative ideas, I recognize the possibility of bias in my own perspective. One thing we have learned from cognitive neuroscience is the fallibility of our minds. Michael Gazzaniga (1998) stated flatly,

> Our mind and brain accomplish the amazing feat of constructing our past and, in so doing, create the illusion of self. . . . The interpreter, the last device in the information chain in our brain, reconstructs the brain events and in doing so makes telling errors of memory, perception, and judgment. (pp. 1–2)

Richard Restak (1994) added,

> Our claims to be "logical" and "reasonable" often mask the operation of modular processes that are inaccessible to our awareness, and persuade us not on the basis of facts but by inducing in us seemingly incontrovertible feelings of certitude. (p. 53)

Optical illusions illustrate the way our brains try to make sense of incomplete sensory information by filling in for what is missing.

As I studied explanations of brain functioning in recent years, I have struggled with the question of what they mean for education, determined not to overstate the implications. Psychologist John Bruer (1997) advised educators not to concern themselves with the physical brain at this point but to focus instead on cognitive science, which he says has more immediate relevance to classroom practice. Many brain researchers take a similar position.

Scientists at an invitational conference I attended, held in 1996 under auspices of the Education Commission of the States, recommended that educators not rush to put new research findings into practice. And although I have talked directly with relatively few neuroscientists, I believe most would probably refrain from endorsing innovative practices supposedly based on their work. Nevertheless I find myself in agreement with the consultants quoted earlier who say brain science, although incomplete, already demonstrates the importance of novelty, interaction, and personal involvement in learning experiences.

WHAT WE'RE LEARNING ABOUT THE BRAIN

Specifically, consider a few statements about brain organization and functioning that can now be made with reasonable assurance:

1. *The brain is modular.* As a result of millions of years of evolution, the human brain "is not a unified neural network that supports general problem solving" (Gazzaniga, 1998, p. 174). It is a collection of learning systems nested together to allow for specific responses to specific challenges. Although researchers do not yet understand how this decentralized system works together to give us consciousness, they have concluded that the brain is not organized hierarchically with functions controlled from a central module (Restak, 1994). Every brain is highly complex, a network of numerous specific capabilities.

2. *Brains change physically in response to experience.* Although human brains are structurally similar, each brain is different, partly because of genetic inheritance and partly because brain organization changes, to some extent, in response to experience. Throughout life, but especially in the very young, brains form more synaptic connections in complex than in unstimulating environments (Diamond & Hopson, 1998).

3. *Emotions play a crucial role in learning.* The brain processes many inputs simultaneously in multiple ways. We pay immediate attention to, and we recall more readily, experiences that have strong emotional overtones (Damasio, 1994; LeDoux, 1996).

Our personal decisions are influenced by our emotions, often unconsciously.

4. *Elaboration strengthens memory*. Memories are not stored whole but are reconstructed by recombining aspects of the original experience. Daniel Schacter (1996), a neuroscientist specializing in memory, wrote that "our recollections are largely at the mercy of our elaborations; only those aspects of experience that are targets of elaborative encoding processes have a high likelihood of being remembered subsequently" (p. 56).

WHAT THESE NEW UNDERSTANDINGS MEAN FOR EDUCATION

We cannot deduce a theory of education from these statements alone. However, like the consultants I quoted earlier, I see findings of this nature as highly consistent with what I know from other sources, including cognitive science, educational research, and my own experience as a teacher and an observer of education. In schools I have visited, I have seen students doing intellectually demanding activities meaningful to them. They were typically in settings where they were expected to show initiative, prepare plans, and actively search for and use information on a topic that aroused their curiosity. I am confident that those students, because of their emotional involvement and their elaborated experiences, will remember and understand the subjects they were studying much better than the many other students I have seen who exhibited no personal connection with, or sense of purpose for, their schooling.

Of course, active engagement in itself does not guarantee that students will learn what they need to know. Productive learning depends on other factors as well (Brandt, 1998), including the nature of the tasks students are assigned and teachers' ability to inspire, explain, demonstrate, inquire, and offer feedback. A report from the prestigious National Academy of Sciences (1999) summarized research on learning as follows:

- Lessons should be tailored to what students already know, deepening and expanding their understanding.

- Curriculum should be designed to help students learn with understanding rather than to memorize disconnected facts and skills.
- Students should get feedback that encourages them to revise and improve the quality of their thinking.
- The setting should create a sense of community that encourages high-quality learning.

To summarize, I am convinced that, when combined with knowledge from other sources, information about brain functioning is consistent with educators' experience that students learn well when they have opportunities to make choices and work actively with others on purposeful projects.

BRAIN RESEARCH APPLIED TO SOCIAL AND EMOTIONAL LEARNING

Our Brain Is a Social Brain

How does this general concept of "brain-compatible" teaching apply to social and emotional learning? Some of the answers can be found by reviewing information about the brain and social and emotional development. As one of their brain–mind principles, Renate Caine and Geoffrey Caine (1997) noted that "the brain is a social brain" and explained it this way:

> Throughout our lives, our brain/minds change in response to their engagement with others—so much so that individuals must always be seen to be integral parts of larger social systems. Indeed, part of our identity depends on establishing community and finding ways to belong. Learning, therefore, is profoundly influenced by the nature of the social relationships within which people find themselves. (pp. 104–105)

Restak (1994) explained that this is so thanks to the growth and enhanced functioning of the frontal lobes. "No other creature," he continued, including the higher primates, comforts the injured or the bereaved, because other creatures cannot imaginatively identify with another. Prehistoric man was also singularly lacking in this capacity to put himself in another's place. With the development of this capacity within our species . . . came the capacity for imaginative identification with others. Societies and organized communities followed. (p. 108)

Brain researchers' views suggest that when discussing education, limitations on the nature and extent to which changes can be effected in students are kept in the forefront. For example, Restak's comments are in connection with his description of how injury to the frontal lobes impedes social interaction. "How curious and sobering it is to realize that our most advanced and evolved mental activities depend on unimpaired functioning of a specific part of the brain." Asked by a high school teacher about students "whose attention span, motivation, autonomy, and emotion appear to be diminished," Restak mused, "Is it possible that many of these children are being deprived directly or indirectly of adequate frontal development because of environmental deficiencies?. . . This question is intriguing but unanswerable" (p. 108). Contending with such problems, teachers can do only what is possible under classroom conditions to make up for what family and community may not have provided.

In addition to underestimating how damage or neglect affect students' social skills, we may have overestimated how much of behavior is learned. Gazzaniga (1998), known for his work with Roger Sperry on right–left brain patients, now takes a decidedly evolutionary perspective, asserting that many brain functions are not, as Jean Piaget claimed, learned through experience. "Instead, so-called learned responses reflect continuing maturation of the brain. We don't learn to talk, as most think. We start to talk when the brain is good and ready to say something" (p. 58). Gazzaniga seems to take delight in being provocative, but his statement accurately reflects the growing influence of evolutionary psychology. If, as evolutionists contend, many aspects of brain functioning are primarily genetic rather than constructed from experience, educators will find it advantageous to work in tune with the brain's built-in capabilities. "We are a finely honed machine that has amazing capacities for learning and inventiveness," Gazzaniga wrote,

> Yet these capacities were not picked up at a local book-store or developed from everyday experience. The abilities to learn and think come with our brains. The knowledge we acquire with these devices results from interactions with our culture. But the devices come with the brain, just as brakes come with a car. (p. 59)

Our Emotions Play a Role in Social and Personal Decisions

Our understanding of emotions has also deepened greatly in recent decades. Antonio Damasio (1994), for example, showed that, contrary to what might be assumed, emotions play an essential role in such mental activities as planning, monitoring, and making personal decisions. These functions are carried out in partnership between the amygdala, which plays a key role in processing of emotions (LeDoux, 1996) and the frontal lobes, which mature very late and which, as Restak observed, are home to the most human of all mental activities and personal and social decision making.

The intimate relationship scientists have discovered between emotions and the decisions that shape our interactions with others shows the appropriateness of the term *social and emotional learning.* This insight, along with the more general observations about brain-compatible schooling I made earlier, lead me to offer three suggestions:

1. *Social and emotional learning should be conducted in accord with what is known about the capabilities and limitations of the human brain.* Stanislaus Dehaene (1997), a French mathematician turned cognitive neuroscientist, referring to complaints on both sides of the Atlantic about poor student performance in mathematics, believes that "our school system is not to blame. Innumeracy has much deeper roots: Ultimately it reflects the human brain's struggle for storing arithmetical knowledge" (p. 138). Based on his knowledge of the brain, Dehaene advised that "bombarding the juvenile brain with abstract axioms is probably useless" (p. 241).

He noted approvingly that in the United States, the National Council of Teachers of Mathematics is now deemphasizing the rote learning of facts and procedures and is focusing instead on teaching an intuitive familiarity with numbers. Describing a successful program for underprivileged children, he said, "The results are remarkable . . . in fact, most children are only too pleased to learn mathematics if only one shows them the playful aspects before the abstract symbolism" (pp. 142–143).

Similarly, social and emotional learning should be taught in accord with what is known about brain functioning. For example, because the brain apparently stores verbal and conceptual knowledge differently from procedural knowledge (such as swimming ability), teachers who wish to teach behavior must give students practice in the necessary skills rather than depending on words alone.

Perhaps the most important insights into human behavior coming from recent brain research are those explaining how emotions affect our thoughts and actions. Discussing implications of his research, Damasio (1994) observesd the following:

> Educational systems might benefit from emphasizing unequivocal connections between current feelings and predicted future outcomes, and that children's overexposure to violence, in real life, newscasts, or through audiovisual fiction, downgrades the value of emotions and feelings in the acquisition and deployment of adaptive social behavior. (p. 247)

Educators might protest that this should be of concern to parents and society in general more than to schools, but Damasio may have been thinking of educators' role as advocates for children and as educators of current and future parents. With increased recognition of the pivotal importance of nutrition, emotional states, and other aspects of nurturing in the earliest years, it seems clear that our society must find ways to give better support to parents of young children, especially those most in need.

2. *To understand themselves better and to manage their own behavior, students should know the capabilities and limitations of their brains.*

Not only should teachers take brain functioning into account in their teaching; they should also help students to understand their own biological natures. For example, knowing that feelings are the tangible indication of emotions that are sometimes otherwise unconscious may help students learn to recognize and deal with emotional upheaval.

Students also should be helped to understand the fascinating relationship between emotions and decision making. Rather than seeing emotions as opposed to rational thought, as the two have been portrayed in the past, they can learn to make use of their emotions when making personal and social decisions. Damasio (1994) cautioned that

> Knowing about the relevance of feelings in the process of reason does *not* suggest that reason is less important than feelings, that it should take a backseat to them or that it should be less cultivated. On the contrary, taking stock of the pervasive role of feelings may give us a chance of enhancing their positive effects and reducing their potential harm. Specifically, without diminishing the orienting value of normal feelings, one would want to protect reason from the weakness that abnormal feelings or the manipulation of normal feelings can introduce in the process of planning and deciding. (p. 146)

Other knowledge about the brain may encourage students to be more tolerant of others. For example, students should know that human memory is unreliable and that when information is incomplete (as it often is) our brains make sense of situations by filling in what seems to be missing. Gazzaniga (1998) warned,

> Nowhere is our automatic brain in more trouble than in recalling the past. The interpreter, working from noisy data, compounds the problem by embellishing on what it does recall. The story remembered on one day becomes part of the memory for the next time it is told. Soon begins a rich narrative about past events. The narrative most likely becomes less accurate and much more elaborate in its detail. The old adage that so and so just can't see it, can't

see he has certain negative features in his personality, is true. He has weaved another tale about himself. (p. 148)

Knowing that all human beings are subject to such distortion should help students recognize that because their perceptions may not be completely accurate, they should try to understand other points of view and negotiate their differences if necessary.

Ironically, the success of efforts to educate children about emotions depends greatly on the students' emotional state. Neuroscientist Candace Pert (1997) explained as follows:

In order for the brain not to be overwhelmed by the constant deluge of sensory input, some sort of filtering system must enable us to pay attention to what our body-mind deems the most important pieces of information and to ignore the others. . . . Our emotions (or the psychoactive drugs that take over their receptors) decide what is worth paying attention to. (p. 146)

3. *Like other school subjects, social and emotional learning will be more effective when students are engaged in personally meaningful activities.* As I admitted earlier, advice to make instruction "personally meaningful" is probably far too broad to be helpful. Nevertheless, it seems apparent that human brains are designed to ignore what seems irrelevant and focus attention on whatever seems more pertinent. Given the way in which strong emotions can dominate people's sense of what is most pressing at any given moment, it is difficult to justify an educational system that does not address students' emotions explicitly and intelligently. This suggests that instruction in social and emotional learning should use interest-enhancing methods such as stories, projects, simulation, and role-playing as much as possible. A particularly intriguing approach is problem-based learning (Torp & Sage 1998), which was first used in medical schools but has also been used successfully in K–12 education. The method depends on development or selection of real or simulated problems to teach curriculum content. Students acquire the intended knowledge and skill in the course of analyzing and attacking the problem from a variety of points of view.

CONCLUDING THOUGHTS: EDUCATORS MUST ACT TO APPLY BRAIN RESEARCH FOR STUDENTS' ACADEMIC, SOCIAL, AND EMOTIONAL LEARNING

Knowing the brain's complexity, and aware that much about it remains mysterious, I have nevertheless offered broad guidelines for education in general and for the conduct of instruction in social and emotional learning. Educational leaders, as well as front-line practicing educators, need to be guided in their work by empirical findings, but they cannot wait for absolute clarification; they must do what they can with what they have now. Unlike researchers, educators must make specific applications of knowledge to large numbers of students day in and day out, drawing on a variety of sources in what are often unpredictable and confusing circumstances.

When we act on partial knowledge, we run the risk of making mistakes, but educators cannot avoid that quandary; we will never know all we need to know. That does not excuse irresponsible or uninformed behavior, but it does mean that, armed with the best available knowledge, we have an obligation to move forward. Brain research, albeit imperfect, is an important part of that knowledge. At this critical time, teachers need to understand and attend to their students' social and emotional needs, their cognitive knowledge and skills, and the way these areas are intertwined. These areas of human functioning are the common province of the same brain, and so what we know about the brain applies in common to these areas. Faced with many competing demands, administrators and policymakers need to support social and emotional learning with training materials, instructional time, continuous professional development, and enthusiastic leadership. As they do these things, all concerned can be reasonably confident that their actions are consistent with current knowledge about the human brain and that we will be providing students with the best academic, social, and emotional learning experiences possible.

REFERENCES

Brandt, R. S. (1998). *Powerful learning*. Alexandria, VA: Association for Supervision and Curriculum Development.

Bruer, J. T. (1997). Education and the brain: A bridge too far. *Educational Researcher, 26*(8), 4–16.

Caine, R. N., & Caine, G. (1997). *Education on the edge of possibility*. Alexandria, VA: Association for Supervision and Curriculum Development.

Damasio, A. R. (1994). *Descartes' error*. New York: Grosset/Putnam.

Dehaene, S. (1997). *The number sense: How the mind creates mathematics*. New York: Oxford University Press.

Diamond, M., & Hopson, J. (1998). *Magic trees of the mind: How to nurture your child's intelligence, creativity, and healthy emotions from birth through adolescence*. New York: Dutton.

Gazzaniga, M. S. (1998). *The mind's past*. Berkeley: University of California Press.

Jensen, E. (1998). *Teaching with the brain in mind*. Alexandria, VA: Association for Supervision and Curriculum Development.

Kovalik, S. (1994). *ITI (Integrated Thematic Instruction): The model*. Kent, WA: Books for Educators.

National Academy of Sciences. (1999). *How people learn: Brain, mind, experience, and school*. Washington, DC: National Academy Press.

LeDoux, J. (1996). *The emotional brain*. New York: Simon & Schuster.

Pert, C. B. (1997). *Molecules of emotion*. New York: Scribner.

Ravitch, D. (1983). *The troubled crusade*. New York: Basic Books.

Restak, R. (1994). *The modular brain*. New York: Scribner.

Schacter, D. L. (1996). *Searching for memory*. New York: Basic Books.

Sousa, D. A. (1998, December 1). Is the fuss about brain research justified? *Education Week*, pp. 52, 35.

Sylwester, R. (1995). *A celebration of neurons: An educator's guide to the human brain*. Alexandria, VA: Association for Supervision and Curriculum Development.

Torp, L., & Sage, S. (1998). *Problems as possibilities*. Alexandria, VA: Association for Supervision and Curriculum Development.

Wolfe, P. (1997, November 9). Thanks for the memory: Applying brain research to the classroom. Presentation at the meeting of the Tennessee Staff Development Council, November 9, Gatlinburg, TN.

PART TWO

Creating Learning Communities by Enhancing Schools' SEL and EQ

Examples From Practice

I NTRODUCTION

If They Can Do It, Why Can't You?

Maurice J. Elias

Harriett Arnold

Cynthia Steiger Hussey

CASEL: THE COLLABORATIVE FOR ACADEMIC, SOCIAL, AND EMOTIONAL LEARNING

The emphasis on best practice in education has no stronger port of call than work in social–emotional learning (SEL) and emotional intelligence (EQ). Few areas in education have been subject to such consistent research and scrutiny. The Collaborative for Academic, Social, Emotional, Learning (www.CASEL.org) was established in 1995 to provide leadership and oversight for the SEL/EQ field. The terms *social and emotional learning* and *emotional intelligence* and their variants show up with ever-increasing frequency as titles of presentations in educational conferences, in education journals, and in the literatures of related fields such as school counseling, school psychology, parenting, and lay administration of schools. The concept of EQ is considered common language, not education or mental health jargon. The business world has jumped on the concept, as exemplified in the creation of the Consortium for Research on Emotional Intelligence in Organizations (CREIO; www.EIConsortium.org) and by the growing international market for publications concerning EQ-related applications in education, parenting, and business.

CASEL'S REVIEW OF SEL PROGRAMS

Part of the work of CASEL in fostering the growth of the SEL/EQ field is an ongoing activity called the CASEL Review of SEL Programs (SELPR; see Chapter 2 for further information on the Review and CASEL). The purpose of the SELPR is to serve as a clearinghouse and resource link for all SEL/EQ programs with some degree of empirical support. That support may take the form of data on attainment of program objectives or evidence that the program has been implemented with a high degree of fidelity to principles of effective implementation that CASEL and others have established.

The SELPR focuses on specific programs from pre-K–12 and describes their various components so that educational administrators can make an informed choice concerning what might be appropriate to meet the needs of their school or schools. The Review looks at the extent to which specific, available programs cover various SEL competencies; address related behavior and health domains such as substance abuse and violence prevention, health promotion, sexual development, citizenship, and academic achievement; and link to family and community. Also examined are parameters of implementation, training requirements, and supports. As noted earlier, links to program contacts and existing implementers are other important features.

SCHOOLWIDE SEL INITIATIVES

Creating schools that are high in EQ and IQ does not occur by bringing in isolated SEL/EQ programs. Developmental and curricular continuity of programs across grade levels is essential. And equally important is that SEL/EQ not be seen as an "add on" but rather as integral to the structure and functioning of a school. For this to take place, schoolwide SEL initiatives are invaluable.

Of great value is involvement of the entire student body, which in particular means special education students. Too often, such students are excluded from SEL/EQ and related prevention efforts. This is not the case in the programs and procedures outlined in Part II. The authors have made commitments to a full concept of inclusion and have extended the SEL/EQ approach to strongly embrace special education settings.

The examples in Part II detail the inception and application of SEL/EQ at all levels, from a school, to a school system, to an entire nation. Each one reflects adaptation to idiosyncratic circumstances, but that is how all successful implementation takes place. The writers hope to provide readers with a vision of SEL/EQ that is both desirable and attainable. They want to stimulate the reader to think, "If they can do it, why can't we?"

C H A P T E R   S I X

Waging Peace in Our Schools

The Resolving Conflict Creatively Program

Linda Lantieri

I do not want a new generation of children with high intelligence quotients and low caring quotients; with sharp competitive edges and dull cooperative instincts; with highly developed computer skills but poorly developed consciences; with gigantic commitment to the big "I," but little sense of responsibility to the bigger "we."

Marian Wright Edelman, President, Children's Defense Fund
(Children's Defense Fund, 2000)

In 1968, Martin Luther King Jr., asked our nation a compelling question: Where do we go from here—chaos or community? This was the same year I began teaching in a fifth-grade classroom in East Harlem. The 37 children in my class had many needs, and many obstacles interfered with their learning. Yet also present in their lives was a sense of community—an unwritten code, reflected by the open doors of churches and the greetings of neighbors, that these were everybody's children. Back then, I could not have imagined that three decades later I would be interviewed for a prime-time television special titled "Kids Killing Kids."

More and more, chaos seems to be replacing community. Who could predict that the 20th century would end with the senseless stream of violence in our schools and communities that has touched all of our young people, from the youngest to the oldest, from the poorest to the most privileged? As we enter a new century, we are faced with a great challenge—how to reclaim our schools, homes, and communities as violence-free growing zones for our children. How will we ensure that our young people feel so cared for that they would never wish to do harm to themselves or anyone else?

CHALLENGES AND OPPORTUNITIES

These challenges offer an unprecedented opportunity. The choices we make now about how to nurture our youth will have critical implications for generations to come. At this time, we seem to be doing the least harm to the most privileged (Comer, 1999). Yet one U.S. government study found that 25% of teenagers, privileged or not, are at risk for failing to cope with the demands in their lives (National Research Council, 1995).

In his groundbreaking book *Emotional Intelligence*, Daniel Goleman summarized 10 years of scientific study on emotions by saying the following:

> Perhaps the most disturbing piece of data in this book comes from a massive survey of parents and teachers and shows a worldwide trend for the present generation of children to be more troubled emotionally than the last: more lonely and depressed, more angry and unruly, more nervous and prone to worry, more impulsive and aggressive. (Goleman, 1995, p. xiii)

One fact is clear: The times have changed and we must face the changes. Young people are coming to school with fear and anger that walks with them right through the metal detectors set up at school doorways. Families today don't have the luxury of spending as much time together as our own parents spent with us, teaching us the lessons of the heart. Our neighborhoods are no longer functional villages, responsive to young people's needs. Children are growing up farther and farther away from a deep sense of community. Instead of spending meaningful time with friends, parents, and neighbors, children in the United States are spending more time glued to a computer screen or a television set.

In our society, there is a deep current—a belief that something is not okay with the way we are living. In the midst of huge advances in technology and brain research, we are struggling to rescue a whole generation of young people who are growing up without the supports they need. We are facing a deep crisis concerning how to rediscover meaningfulness and purpose, and although we are aware of the void, we have few ideas about what to do.

THE MISSION OF EDUCATION EXPANDS: SCHOOLS PLAY A VITAL ROLE

Fortunately, we know more and more about how education can help young people develop the convictions and skills to take part in shaping a safe, sustainable, and just society. For a long time, schools have performed a socializing function in our society. They are now among the few places—in our fractured times— where young people of diverse backgrounds can be found in large numbers on a daily basis. Schools can give children the opportunity to develop their critical thinking skills, practice handling their emotions, deal with conflicts nonviolently, and rediscover their purpose and vision—if the schools are organized correctly.

Addressing young people's social, emotional, and ethical lives is an immediate, pressing, and urgent need. The mission of our schools is being expanded to include the critical human skills and values our children need for their lives to be safer, happier, and healthier. The definition of a well-educated person is one who possesses an education of the heart and spirit as well as the mind.

For more than three decades, I have devoted my life to the important role schools can play in nurturing the emotional, social, and ethical development of young people. I have been attempting to answer the following question: How can schools help reclaim the hearts and spirits of our youth? I have used my experiences as a former teacher and school administrator while working with a particular initiative, the Resolving Conflict Creatively Program (RCCP), of which I am one of the cofounders.

The RCCP began in 1985 as a collaboration between Educators for Social Responsibility (ESR), Metropolitan (New York) Area, and the New York City Board of Education. Today, the ESR National Center supports efforts to replicate RCCP nationwide. We are now working in more than 400 schools in 16 school districts throughout the country, serving 6,000 teachers and 175,000 young people.

WEAPONS OF THE SPIRIT

The 175,000 young people in RCCP are not armed with the thousands of guns that are still brought into schools on a daily basis or the daily taunts that so many young people wield like weapons. They use weapons of the spirit—creative communication, appreciation for diversity, the ability to center themselves and manage their anger, and skills to resolve conflict nonviolently. These young people attend schools with an educational vision that recognizes that the ability to manage emotions, resolve conflict, and interrupt bias are fundamental skills—skills that can and must be taught.

Despite the fact that there was actually only a one in two million chance of being killed in a school in 1998–1999 and that there has been a 40% decline in school-associated deaths from violence over the past several years, 71% of Americans believe that a shooting is likely to occur in schools (News Distorts Youth, 2001). The people implementing our program do not believe that violence is a necessary risk in going to school. Instead, these folks are talking about the ways they are creating a "culture of nonviolence," in which true school reform and renewal is taking place by addressing human relationships.

RCCP: THE PEACEABLE SCHOOL MODEL

RCCP is one of the nation's largest and longest running, research-based school programs in social and emotional learning focusing in the areas of conflict resolution and diversity education. RCCP's goal is to promote caring and cooperative learning environments by reaching young people through the adults who relate to them on a daily basis in school, at home, and in their communities. It moves beyond implementing an isolated educational innovation and instead seeks to change the entire school culture and beyond, engaging the broader community in creating a safe haven for children.

RCCP uses a broadly conceived strategy to create schools that are peaceable and effective communities of learning. It is characterized by deep, committed involvement over a number of years. The kindergarten through eighth grade part of the model includes the following components:

- *Professional development for teachers* involves a 24-hour introductory course and ongoing support for implementation of the RCCP curriculum through on-site classroom visits.
- *Classroom instruction* features curricula developed in close collaboration with participating teachers.
- *Peer mediation* trains carefully selected groups of students to serve their schools as peer mediators.
- *Administrator training* introduces administrators to the concepts and skills of conflict resolution and bias awareness and explores how their leadership can enhance effective implementation of the program.
- *Parent training* helps parents develop better ways of dealing with conflict and prejudice at home and become more effective leaders in their children's schools.
- *Support staff training* offers an orientation to the skills and concepts of social and emotional learning to build communication skills and conflict resolution among secretaries, cafeteria staff members, bus drivers, and other school support staff.
- *Training of trainers* builds school district capacity to implement independently all program components and to integrate and institutionalize the program into school district curriculum frameworks.

In high schools, RCCP uses another ESR program called Partners in Learning, which includes the following components:

- *Planning and needs assessment* builds collaborative partnerships among the different constituencies in high schools (students, staff members, parents, and community members).
- *Professional development for teachers* includes a 24-hour introductory course in creating and managing peaceable classroom environments. It prepares teachers to implement "best practices" that help strengthen social and emotional competencies, build a cooperative learning environment, and develop more effective communication and problem-solving skills. This is followed by ongoing coaching, consulting, and team building.
- *Classroom instruction* fosters skill instruction in conflict resolution, anger management, and intergroup relations through specific elective courses, as well as through integration into subject areas.
- *Student leadership training and youth development* provides young people with the skills and convictions to participate fully in creating democratic and peaceful classrooms, schools, and communities.

TRANSFORMING SCHOOL CULTURE

Peaceable schools are places where we are able to practice building democratic communities. Schools can be the first training ground for students to develop the habits, values, and behavior needed to participate fully in our diverse society. If they are intentional about it, schools can nurture the development of social responsibility, cooperative problem solving, and nonadversarial dialogue.

Consider the dynamics of this classroom: Mrs. Frye sits at her desk in the back. The front right corner of the classroom bears a multicolored sign that students made, designating the area as "The Peace Corner." Several students are busily working there. Others work quietly with their groups at their tables. Suddenly, Frank, a short boy at the table near the door, breaks the silence.

"Hey, give me back my book, Tom. I know you took it!"

"I don't have your stupid book," Tom responds in a shrill voice. "This is mine." They continue to yell at each other until Sara, a student mediator, walks over and asks, "Would you like me to help?" For a brief moment the boys stop bickering.

By this time, Mrs. Frye is standing behind the two angry boys. Turning to them, she says, "I'd like you both to calm down and decide whether you'd like to discuss this with me or whether you'd like a mediation."

The two boys, still angry, stalk off to different sides of the room. They both know the procedure. They sit apart for a while and calm themselves before they attempt to resolve the conflict; then they walk over to the class mediator for help. During the 3 or 4 minutes that this argument lasted, other students looked on, but continued to work at their tables.

In this RCCP classroom and others like it, staff and students use mediation and negotiation, and discipline is not just a matter of teacher-made edicts. The children know that their job is to express and manage their anger appropriately. They also know that neither physically aggressive behavior nor hurtful, painful words and put-downs are tolerated because students take part in agreement making. They know what happens if agreements are broken, and they have the skills they need to resolve conflicts nonviolently and to encourage their peers to do the same. The children are the peacemakers.

Through involvement in RCCP, young people discover that heroism can take the form of a passionate search for nonviolent solutions to complex problems. This message is exemplified in the comments of a high school sophomore from an RCCP school in California:

> You want respect, but there's only one way that you see you can get that respect, and that's by being tough, bold. That's the way I got respect, by being an aggressive person. I've changed a lot. It's the way I look at people now, listen to them, and talk to them. It's a different kind of high and it feels good.

Kim Jones, RCCP parent and ESR program associate in New York City, illustrates a parent's perspective on the program:

If we demonstrate peaceful responses, our children start to learn by example. Children don't always do what you say, but often what you do. A product of my involvement is that I am trying to "example" the behavior I expect from my children.

And what do the school leaders who are charged with implementing RCCP think about the program and its effects? Lee Ann Crumbley, former principal of an elementary school in Anchorage, Alaska, offers her impression:

RCCP works and takes time. I credit the program with being the major influence on the staff and students of our school in bringing about positive change. The culture of the school has changed over the past 5 years, and our reality now closely matches our expectation in terms of attitudes and behaviors.

EVALUATING RCCP'S EFFECTIVENESS

A recently completed independent evaluation of RCCP schools in New York City, initiated by ESR's New York chapter, provides new evidence of the potential of such efforts in schools (Aber, Brown, & Henrich, 1999). The study, one of the largest scientific evaluations of a school social and emotional learning program ever conducted, involved more than 5,000 children and 300 teachers from 15 public elementary schools over a 2-year period. It was conducted by the National Center for Children in Poverty (NCCP) at the Joseph L. Mailman School of Public Health at Columbia University.

The study found that compared with children who had little or no exposure to the curriculum, children receiving substantial RCCP instruction from their classroom teachers (on average, 25 lessons during the school year) developed in more positive ways. They perceived their social world in a less hostile way, saw violence as an unacceptable option, and chose nonviolent ways to resolve conflict. The most positive change occurred in children who received the most consistent instruction over a 2-year period. Children in this "high lesson group" received significantly increased ratings from their teachers on positive social behaviors and emotional control. Additional results indicated that RCCP benefits all children, regardless of gender, grade level, or risk status. In addition, children who received substantial instruction in the RCCP curriculum performed significantly better on standardized academic achievement tests than did children who had no or little RCCP involvement.

Metis Associates, using a self-evaluation model, also evaluated RCCP in our Atlanta site during the 1996–1997 school year (Metis Associates, 1998). The assessment shows that RCCP has had a positive impact on program participants. According to Stanley Schneider, the principal investigator, "The changes in measures we observed throughout the year of the evaluation were greater than one would expect in such a short time" (p. 16). Among the key findings were that 64% of teachers reported less physical violence in the classroom; 75% of teachers reported an increase in student cooperation; 92% of the students felt better about themselves; and more than 90% of parents reported an increase in their own communication and problem-solving skills. Administrative data from the Atlanta evaluation show that student attendance rates improved and that there was a lower rate of course failure. The in-school and out-of-school suspension rates at the RCCP middle school decreased significantly, whereas among non-RCCP middle schools, rates increased during the same period. At the RCCP high school, dropout rates decreased significantly, whereas rates in non-RCCP high schools increased during the same period.

ADVOCATING FOR A SHIFT IN APPROACHING STANDARDS IN EDUCATION

Although RCCP is one of the largest and longest running programs in social and emotional learning, our 400 schools represent only a small fraction of all the schools in this country. We have been successful in reaching thousands of young people, yet we also recognize that this is not enough. As Lisbeth Schorr says in her book *Common Purpose*, "We have learned to create the small exceptions that can change the lives of hundreds. But we have not learned how to make the exceptions the rule to change the lives of millions" (1997, p. xiii).

Successful models of social and emotional learning programs in a variety of school districts (urban, suburban, and rural) provide concrete examples and help this become feasible. There is growing public awareness of the idea that emotional intelligence (EQ) is as important, if not more so, than IQ in terms of future success—both personal and professional. This vision of education must become the rule rather than the exception.

As the debate around national standards continues in this country, we realize that we are still addressing only half the story. A young person can do well in school and flunk in life. To date, the talk around national standards has rarely addressed the social, emotional, and ethical domain in a comprehensive way. We need standards for young people's social, emotional, and ethical development that are as rigorous as those for the cognitive and intellectual domains.

If we are successful in promoting policy changes that include integrating the skills and competencies of SEL into national standards and state curriculum frameworks, then we can begin to look at reordering resources toward more preventive approaches that focus on the development of the whole child.

AN EMERGING PARADIGM CHANGE

As the social and emotional learning movement continues to grow and deepen in schools, we are also operating in a wider context of change. There are clear indicators that a new paradigm is emerging in how we think and what we value—a new model emphasizing personal growth and community rather than personal autonomy and mobility. It focuses on cooperation rather than cutthroat competition. The paradigm represents a change in human consciousness. Looking at this shift, it becomes clear that the skills and concepts that are taught in a program such as RCCP are the competencies needed to bring us into the 21st century. And as we take part in preparing young people to play a role in this transformation, I am acutely aware that it will not be easy.

We adults have to change our education priorities dramatically for this to happen. We are a country that has let its priorities become so skewed, we spend $4 billion in medical care each year to take care of gunshot wounds and still don't guarantee every child health care coverage. In fact, among all the industrial countries, the United States ranks first in military exports and defense expenditures and last in protecting children against gun violence. A gun takes the life of a child in this country every 2 hours. We must invest in the support communities need to address this grim statistic: One out of five children grows up poor—more than 13 million children across the country. We are living in a country that spends more money on prisons than education, that guarantees young people the availability of a prison cell but not a college education. And the wealth of only three of the richest people in the United States exceeds the gross national product of the 32 least developed countries. The annual budget of the Head Start programs pales in the shadow of spending on military weaponry (Children's Defense Fund, 2000).

What would it cost to implement a comprehensive social and emotional learning program in every school in this country for 1 year? The price tag is $4 billion. Can we find this money through a decrease in defense spending, by controlling access to guns so we will not need to spend as much money to treat gunshot wounds, and by limiting the salary of top executives to perhaps the two digit, instead of three digit, millions? It does not seem impossible. And it may be among the best investments we can make toward spending less on the consequences of violence and more on nurturing the social, ethical, and emotional development of our children.

VISION FOR THE FUTURE

We know we will have succeeded when programs such as RCCP are no longer needed, when this broader vision of education is widely adapted and supported. Until then, recalling the words of the Reverend Martin Luther King Jr., we "keep our eyes on the prize and carry on."

Yet schools working alone cannot make a big enough dent in the crisis we face as a nation. Even if we could effect a comprehensive, multiyear commitment to the teaching of emotional and social competencies and conflict resolution skills in every school in the United States, we would still be unable to turn the tide. As those of us who are involved with programs such as RCCP wage peace in our schools, our children are getting strong, frequent, and extreme messages to the contrary from the wider society and from their own communities. They have ready access to real and simulated violence. Some live in homes and neighborhoods where violence is often the accepted norm.

Thus our response to these complicated issues must be a wide-ranging and public one. It must be part of a larger movement of social change and activism with the ultimate goal of bringing stability, community, love, and safety into children's lives. That movement must involve the private sector, national and local governments, businesses, community organizations, religious groups, law enforcement, and researchers to bring about the kind of heart-to-heart resuscitation that will transform neighborhoods into functional villages again. Peaceful classrooms and schools are more than refuges from harm—they are interdependent models for the greater community.

In our long-term vision, we see children entering kinder-garten and immediately beginning to learn that differences are accepted, that feelings are okay, and that conflict can be resolved nonviolently. By the time they are in first or second grade, these young people will almost automatically choose conflict resolution skills to mediate disputes among classmates. Later, as they enter high school, they will have the courage and skills to stand up to bigotry and violence and to work for a more peaceful, caring, and just society. When young people can experience this way of being in their schools, the chances that they will fully internalize and employ this approach throughout their adults lives will be much, much greater.

Will we learn from the mistakes of the past so that we can avoid losing more of our young people? More and more schools are making significant long-term commitments to creating cultures that emphasize caring, respect, and safety. Our willingness to turn schools into caring communities rather than armed fortresses may determine the future of young people in far greater ways than we know. As 1999 drew to a close, I had the extraordinary opportunity to be present at the final meeting of the century of the United Nations' General Assembly. It was inspiring to witness the UN declare the first decade of the new millennium as the "Decade of the Culture of Peace and Nonviolence for the Children of the World." Our work is clearly cut out for us in meeting this challenge.

NONVIOLENCE AS THE NORM

While visiting one of our RCCP elementary schools recently, I witnessed two fourth-grade boys in an intensive conversation as they were walking in front of me, oblivious that I was behind them. One of the boys had his arm around the shoulder of the other boy, who was visibly upset. "He said those mean words to you?" asked the one boy. "Yes," the other one nodded. "And he even almost hit you?" Another affirmative nod from the troubled youngster. "I know what must be happening," said his friend. "That mean boy is probably new to the school. He doesn't know that we don't do things like that around here." The power of non-violence had taken hold so strongly that these students could not imagine why someone had been acting mean except that "he was new to the school." To make such schools the norm, not the exception, is an aspiration worthy of our greatest efforts and the resources, time, and commitment that will be needed. It will be worth it.

REFERENCES

Aber, J. L., Brown, J. L., & Henrich, C. C. (1999). *Teaching conflict resolution: An effective school-based approach to violence prevention* [Research brief]. New York: Columbia University, Joseph L. Mailman School of Public Health, National Center for Children in Poverty.

Children's Defense Fund. (2000). *The state of America's children 2000.* Washington, DC: Author.

Comer, J. (1999, November 6). *Social and emotional learning and digital technologies: New means and methods.* Remarks at the Social and Emotional Learning Fall 1999 Conference. New York: Teachers College, Project for Social and Emotional Learning.

Goleman, D. (1995). *Emotional intelligence.* New York: Bantam.

Metis Associates. (1998). *Atlanta Public Schools: Resolving Conflict Creatively Program. Final evaluation report, 1996–1997.* New York: Author.

National Research Council, Panel on High-Risk Youth (1995). *Losing generations.* Washington, DC: National Academy Press.

News distorts youth, reports say. (2001, May). *Youth Today,* 5.

Schorr, L. (1997). *Common purpose: Strengthening families and neighborhoods to rebuild America.* New York: Doubleday.

CHAPTER SEVEN

Building Capacity From Within

Changing the Adult Working Environment in Our Schools

Sharon Rose Powell

Margo R. Ross

To exercise leadership today, leaders must institutionalize their leadership. . . . They must create or strengthen systems that survive them.

John W. Gardner (1995)

Strengthening the U.S. school system has been the focus of a frenzy of national reform activity in recent years.

Economic, social, and political trends, including the increasingly competitive but volatile global economy and changing demographics of the U.S. population, continue to propel fundamental changes in American schools (Murphy & Adams, 1998). Many of these changes have led to strong and persistent criticisms of education in this country (Trimble & Miller, 1996), and demands for more effective leadership and greater cohesiveness among those working in schools.

This chapter provides school leaders with practical, specific exercises designed to address these demands. We offer readers detailed descriptions of activities that School Leadership Teams have found useful in transforming an often mundane ritual, the faculty meeting, into a time of "reunion and renewal" for staff. Concrete examples are given that illustrate how teams have used these activities in their own schools to increase cooperation and collegiality among faculty, improve school climate and staff morale, and develop and institutionalize healthy practices. With increasing demands for improved school leadership, guidelines like these have never been more valuable, relevant, and timely.

BACKGROUND

Responding to a variety of criticisms of the modern American school system, educational reformers have long called for improved leadership for our schools (Murphy & Hallinger, 1992). Administrators who were trained to be managers are now expected to be leaders, with such responsibilities as creating shared visions, developing collaborative decision-making processes, enabling teacher success, fostering collaborative team relationships, and promoting teacher development (Neufeld, 1997). Strong collaborative skills have surpassed strong bureaucratic skills as important qualities needed for effective school leaders (Payzant & Gardner, 1994). These changes have dramatically highlighted the importance of participatory leadership and administrators' interpersonal skills as they promote staff ownership of change and create an effective internal support structure (Murphy & Hallinger, 1992).

Practicing administrators themselves have repeatedly noted personal needs to develop a new set of knowledge and skills essential for effectiveness as leaders in education today. Goddard (1997) surveyed 193 principals in Nova Scotia regarding their priorities for professional development and training opportunities. The most frequent responses included requests for techniques for increasing positive community involvement, techniques for improving staff relations, and strategies for building school culture and climate.

Similarly, Neufeld (1997) examined the perceptions of 23 urban middle school principals regarding their needs for professional development and training. These administrators spoke specifically about desiring additional knowledge and skills around the meaning and practice of leadership and the creation of a positive school culture. For example, they understood the importance of engaging teachers and others in creating a shared vision for their schools but did not know how to accomplish this task. They acknowledged a responsibility for facilitating goal setting, problem solving, and team building but were lacking the knowledge and skills necessary to address these issues effectively. Varner (1998) described the frustration that teachers experience when their principal is not knowledgeable about their needs. She suggested that principals must learn how to lead people through change and how to run highly efficient and effective meetings that get all the issues on the table.

Administrators, researchers, and reformers are increasingly recognizing the critical need for school leaders to "create and strengthen systems that survive them." One strategic method for addressing this need, which has emerged as a common theme throughout the research, is the development of effective school management teams. Creating and maintaining collaborative, competent teams of administrators, faculty, and parents contribute to a positive school climate and culture, and to the development of a shared vision for schools. In addition, "creating and sustaining effective [management] teams may provide an answer to the shortcomings of large schools and the isolation of teachers and students" (Trimble & Miller, 1996, p. 36). According to Lambert (1998b), building school-based leadership capacity is critical if we are to maintain and improve the strength and commitment of educators. For the past 14 years, the Princeton Center for Leadership Training has been building the capacity of schools and school personnel to develop and maintain effective school management teams, also referred to as School Leadership Teams or Action Teams.

The work of the Princeton Center reflects a belief that building a strong foundation of healthy relationships among faculty, administrators, and parents is at the core of school reform. If this element is missing, it can disrupt or even prevent a school from instituting necessary changes. Creating a healthy social and emotional working environment for teachers must become a top priority before they can institute significant improvements in their students' learning environment.

WHAT CONSTITUTES A HEALTHY WORKING ENVIRONMENT?

Members of a school's faculty constitute a group; they are a collection of individuals sharing certain common circumstances. Like all groups, faculty will progress through a set of developmental stages—forming, norming, storming, and performing. Schools that pay attention to these stages and establish rituals and other healthy practices on an ongoing basis reap the benefits of high teacher morale, cooperative and collegial professionals with a shared passion for teaching and learning, and a climate that supports risk-taking and "reflective" conversation.

Redesign Faculty Meetings

One practical way to introduce these healthy practices, and to give school personnel time to experience and reflect on these practices, is by redesigning faculty meetings. Most schools hold faculty meetings for at least 1 hour each month, yet few attendees value these sessions or use them to promote more positive working relationships among faculty and administrators.

School Leadership Teams can develop the skills and knowledge necessary to lead their faculty through a process of "reunion and renewal." Using the four group stages as a guide, faculty meetings can be restructured to introduce new practices, with time for small group exchange, debate, dialogue, and reflection.

Forming

Most veteran staff members remember what it was like when they first joined the faculty of their school. An exercise titled "Reviewing Our History: Then and Now" gives staff members an opportunity to share significant events and turning points throughout the school's history—usually from the 1960s to the present. A time line is placed on one wall of the room, and teams of teachers and administrators place their initials on the year that they first began working at the school, along with a descriptive phrase that depicts their first impressions of it. Then, anywhere along the continuum that significant events occurred, staff members describe what happened (and when) that affected the climate of the school. Next, beginning with the most veteran member of the school, a story unfolds about each member's experiences, building on the central themes that become apparent as the collective history is shared. Following this exercise, staff members have an opportunity to step back and reflect on how people's relationships were formed and how events have affected those relationships over time. Historical patterns emerge that continue to affect the climate and culture of the school, and faculty can take notice and agree to let go of destructive forces from the past while building on strengths and reinforcing positive events.

One such example was the realization from the staff of an urban middle school that they were still mourning the loss of two students and a faculty member who were killed in separate accidents more than 10 years ago. These traumatic events, all occurring within several years of each other, rocked the foundation of the school, and the faculty had never recovered. The faculty had become cautious and distrustful and unwilling to invest in collaborative professional endeavors. "Reviewing Our History" was a much-needed wake-up call for the faculty that resulted in a cathartic grieving and letting-go process, followed by a reemergence of commitment and passion for teaching.

Norming

Faculty meetings can also be a place to review a set of internal norms and staff practices that affect the way people get along and work together. One exercise that can help faculty assess their

Figure 7.1   Exercise: How Are We Doing?

How Are We Doing?

An Assessment of Our School's Norms and Healthy Practices

Directions: Consider the following internal norms and healthy practices for staff. Identify three areas of strength and three that need work.

- The way we communicate
- The way people treat each other
- The way we begin each day
- The way we end each day
- The way conflicts or problems are handled
- The way staff is assigned to tasks
- The way decisions are made
- Work standards
- Attendance
- Planning time
- Faculty meetings
- Faculty inservice
- Professional development opportunities
- Others:

---

school's culture and climate is called "How Are We Doing?" (Figure 7.1). Interdisciplinary teams of faculty identify three practices that they value and appreciate and three practices that need work. Teams collect examples of how each practice is played out and the effect it has on the working environment. Teams report their findings to the entire faculty and, collectively, the practices that need the most work are identified. Teams then brainstorm ways that new rituals can be introduced to address the areas that need work. For example, a faculty in one large high school noted that the way they began each day felt isolating and unfriendly— both for staff and students. By introducing a new ritual, piped-in soft classical music throughout the school for the first 5 minutes of the day, everyone felt more relaxed and connected to one another.

Figure 7.2   Exercise: Straight Talk With Colleagues

Straight Talk With Colleagues

	Name of person receiving feedback	What I appreciate	What gets in the way	What I need from you
Person 1				
Person 2				
Person 3				
Person 4				

Storming

In many schools, faculty and administrators get stuck around "storming" issues, holding on to grievances, insults, and disappointments for months and even years. Imagine a school climate that supports the belief "we agree to disagree"; a climate that fosters sharing diverse perspectives on teaching and learning; and an atmosphere that supports opportunities for colleagues to give and receive constructive feedback. Faculty meetings are an excellent place to hold periodic "Straight Talk" sessions, a practice that can address storming issues directly and, in many cases, prevent long-term storming conflicts from escalating and becoming a destructive force among the faculty. "Straight Talk" involves identifying one to five colleagues who agree to provide each other with feedback. First, each person writes down all of the things that he or she appreciates about each member participating in the process. Then he or she identifies (a) what is getting in the way of their working relationships and (b) what he or she needs from the other person to strengthen the professional bond. With Straight Talk forms completed (see Figure 7.2), one member of the group receives feedback from each person, in turn, without any interruptions, except asking for clarification, if needed.

After a person has received feedback from all members of the group, the feedback recipient summarizes what he or she heard others say and thanks group members for sharing. At no time do members of feedback teams explain their behavior or get into conversations about what they heard. By practicing Straight Talk on a regular basis in a structured setting, staff members learn, firsthand, the effect they have on others and can modify behavior and attitudes, should they want to respond to constructive feedback.

This process is most useful for members of an academic team or long-standing committee. When members of a staff become more adept at giving and receiving this kind of feedback, it begins to occur more frequently as a matter of course in day-to-day operations of the school. In some cases, faculty may want to expand this process to include participating in a more comprehensive, 360-degree feedback exercise that assesses colleagues in the areas of job knowledge, planning and organization, initiative and resourcefulness, professionalism, dependability, teamwork, and communication.

Performing

Schools are in the business of performing; unfortunately, school personnel are asked more and more to perform new tasks in record time with limited resources. On top of this, we have now added the expectation that faculty and administrators will collaborate on everything from designing a new curriculum to restructuring the way they use time, space, and resources in schools. It is not surprising that frustration is high when the people involved in shared decision making lack the tools to plan and communicate effectively in teams.

One way to illustrate "what can go wrong" with school team efforts is the exercise "Blindfold Adventure." The task is simple: Everyone (up to 20–30 people on a team) is blindfolded and cannot speak while forming a straight line in reverse-alphabetical order by first names. The scene is predictable: Some people stand frozen, waiting to be rescued. Others latch on to anyone and get into some semblance of a line—not caring what the order looks like. A few brave souls may try to organize the group by attempting to create a system of communicating, for example, drawing the first letter of their names on the hands or backs of participants. This activity gives people an opportunity to create order from chaos, although the many obstacles placed in their way make their goal difficult to achieve.

The learning comes when the blindfolds are removed and a discussion ensues:

- How would you describe the way this group worked together to accomplish its task?
- What are some of the obstacles that got in the way; how were these obstacles similar to or different from those we face in collaborative decision-making efforts at school?
- What kinds of leadership emerged during this exercise; what was missing?
- What have we learned from this experience about the essential ingredients needed to work effectively on teams?

Have More Participatory Faculty Meetings

Faculty meetings can give staff time to practice their problem-solving and communication skills by introducing familiar hands-on activities. In the "Building Bridges" exercise, teams have a limited amount of time to construct a bridge using only straws and straight pins. The bridge has to be strong enough to support a person's shoe while also being evaluated on its beauty and originality. Sometimes leaders are assigned a specific role that affects the dynamics of the group.

In "Broken Squares," team members are each given an envelope with geometric shapes in it. The goal for the group is to create a square of equal size for each member. Without talking, members may share their pieces of the puzzle with others, but they cannot ask for or take another piece, even though they may need it to carry out the task. In both of these examples, teams share a common experience while discovering their multiple talents, individual areas of expertise, and the benefits of using their collective emotional intelligence to reach common goals—important lessons for real-life problem-solving efforts in the future.

CONCLUSION

If leaders in education are to respond effectively to increasing demands to strengthen the school system, they must recognize the potential for improvement that already exists within the school structure. They can "strengthen systems that survive them" by introducing and developing healthy practices that address the needs of faculty in a naturally occurring forum—the faculty meeting. Through small but strategic changes in a common routine, school leaders can infuse the climate and culture of our schools with ongoing opportunities for collaboration, team building, support, reflection, and growth.

Attending to the stages of group development with practices such as those described here allows School Leadership Teams to change the agenda of faculty meetings. They become places for teachers and administrators to exchange ideas, review strengths, identify areas that need work in their professional working environment, and experience firsthand how to solve challenging problems in a collaborative spirit. As faculty meetings take on these new purposes, educators' roles and functions begin to transform. "As roles change, relationships change. People see each other in a new light. They recognize new skills and resources in people they have known for years" (Lambert, 1998a, p. 20). These changes begin the process of reunion and renewal within the adult working environment of the school. There is no better way to have a significant impact on student learning environments than to do just that—to build the capacity from within.

REFERENCES

Gardner, J. W. (1990). *On leadership.* New York: Free Press.

Goddard, J. T. (1997, March). *Voices from the swamp: Identifying the professional development needs of principals.* Paper presented at the annual meeting of the American Educational Research Association. (ERIC Document Reproduction Service No. ED 406 752)

Lambert, L. (1998a). *Building leadership capacity in schools.* Alexandria, VA: Association for Supervision and Curriculum Development.

Lambert, L. (1998b). How to build leadership capacity. *Educational Leadership,* ASCD, 17–19.

Murphy, J., & Adams, J. E., Jr. (1998). Reforming America's schools: 1980–2000. *Journal of Educational Administration, 36,* 426–444.

Murphy, J., & Hallinger, P. (1992). The principalship in an era of transformation. *Journal of Educational Administration, 30*(3), 77–88.

Neufeld, B. (1997). Responding to the expressed needs of urban middle school principals. *Urban Education, 31,* 490–509.

Payzant, T. W., & Gardner, M. (1994). Changing roles and responsibilities in a restructuring school district. *NASSP Bulletin, 78*(560), 8–17.

Trimble, S., & Miller, J. W. (1996). Creating, invigorating, and sustaining effective teams. *NASSP Bulletin, 80*(584), 35–40.

Varner, E. (1998). The mark of leadership: Principals need professional development, too! *Middle Ground, 2*(2), 27–28.

CHAPTER EIGHT

Building Community in School

The Child Development Project

Catherine Lewis

Marilyn Watson

Eric Schaps

W hen second-grade teacher Ruby Tellsworth returned to her classroom after a break, she was surprised to find that her students had convened a class meeting and were intently discussing a problem that had come up during recess. They listened carefully to one another's ideas and solved the problem while she observed from the sidelines (Kohn, 1990).

How did second-graders learn to solve a playground conflict without help from an adult? Why did they take responsibility to call a class meeting and, even without an adult present, endeavor to treat one another respectfully? "Discipline," in most educational writing, connotes student obedience and the methods to elicit it. But "discipline" can mean something quite different: the qualities of heart and mind that will enable children to sustain a humane, caring society. The second-graders who spontaneously cut short recess to solve a class problem already show many of these qualities: a sense of responsibility for problems that threaten the common good, willingness to take initiative in solving these problems, and some skills (such as convening a community meeting and listening to each other) needed to work collaboratively toward solutions. Helping students to develop these qualities is the focus of the Child Development Project.

PROGRAM OVERVIEW

The Child Development Project (CDP) is a comprehensive elementary school improvement program designed to help children develop both the skills and the inclinations to be respectful, responsible, and caring. The CDP helps schools to foster students' social, emotional, and ethical development in concert with their academic growth. Specifically, the CDP helps educators to reshape many aspects of the school environment around four basic principles:

1. Build warm, stable, supportive relationships among and between students, teachers, and parents.

2. Provide regular opportunities for students to collaborate with others.

3. Provide regular opportunities for students to exercise "voice and choice" (i.e., influence and autonomy).

4. Articulate, discuss, and encourage reflection on core values and ideals.

To help teachers bring these principles to life, the CDP offers strategies, materials, and professional development aimed at building students' sense of community in the classroom and school. The term *sense of community* refers not to knowing the surrounding neighborhood, but rather to students' feelings of being cared about and influential in school and of being valued school members. In its emphasis on supportive interpersonal relationships, sense of community overlaps with the terms *belongingness* and *connectedness*, which are also used in the literature (e.g., Resnick et al., 1997). But it also reflects students' sense of "voice and choice," that is, their sense of influence and autonomy in the classroom and school at large. For reasons explained below, we have come to believe that bolstering sense of community in school is one of the most important goals that a school improvement effort can address.

The CDP program consists of the following mutually supporting components designed to affect daily life in the classroom, in the school at large, and in the connections between home and school:

- *Class meetings.* Class meetings provide a useful forum for students and their teacher to set class goals, norms, and ground rules; to make plans and decisions; and to discuss and resolve issues and problems. Class meetings help to build unity and a sense of shared purpose and help students learn the skills of group participation and collaboration. Several forms of class meetings are described in the book *Ways We Want Our Class to Be* (Child Development Project, 1996), along with suggestions for starting the year, facilitating effective meetings, and deepening students' skills over time.
- *Cooperative learning.* The CDP's approach to cooperative learning is similar to a number of other approaches in that students work in pairs or small groups to deepen both their understanding of subject matter and their capacity to work together effectively and respectfully. The emphasis is not just on what students learn academically, but on how they work together. Where CDP differs from some other cooperative learning approaches is in its avoidance of intergroup competition, extrinsic group rewards, group grades, and preassigned group roles (e.g., facilitator, encourager). The CDP framework for cooperative learning and a variety of

specific cooperative learning formats are contained in the book *Blueprints for a Collaborative Classroom* (Child Development Project, 1997).

- *Developmental discipline.* This approach to discipline and classroom management is based on the recognition that children develop social skills and moral understanding in much the same way they learn academic skills and concepts. It emphasizes relationship building and a proactive "teaching" approach to discipline rather than efficiency and control. Teachers are encouraged to use unity-building activities and to control misbehavior in nonpunitive ways. The book *Among Friends: Classrooms Where Caring and Learning Prevail* (Dalton & Watson, 1997), describes the rationale and general approach of developmental discipline. The book *Mrs. Ecken, Do You Like Me? Building Nurturing Relationships With Other People's Children* (Watson, 2002), describes in detail the unfolding of developmental discipline in one teachers inner-city elementary classroom.

- *Literature-based reading.* Two values-rich, literature-based reading programs, Reading, Thinking, and Caring (for grades K–3) and Reading for Real (for grades 4–8), foster students' motivation to read and their development as principled, caring people. Central to these programs are 250 multicultural books, which are used as teacher read-alouds or as "partner-reads" by pairs of students. A teacher's guide for each book summarizes its main ideas and themes, offers discussion questions, and suggests engaging writing and follow-up activities.

- *Cross-grade "buddies" activities.* Whole classes of older and younger students come together every week or two, and each older student pairs up with his or her younger "buddy" for an academic or recreational activity. Buddy pairs are assigned for the entire year, so that powerful cross-age relationships can develop, important social skills can be learned, and a caring ethos can be created in the school. The book *That's My Buddy* (Child Development Project, 2001), provides advice on how to set up buddy programs and prepare students for them, describes the types of activities that work well in the buddies context, and suggests ways of deepening the learning that occurs via buddies activities.

- *Home-involvement activities.* These are short conversational activities that students do at home with a parent or other caregiver. Eighteen activities per grade level (K–6), in both English and Spanish, provide parents and children with opportunities to share ideas and experiences, while also offering parents a window on what their child is learning at school. Presented in reproducible form in a series of seven Homeside Activities books, these activities promote student communication skills, help them to learn more about their parents' lives and perspectives, and validate the family's culture and traditions.
- *Whole school community-building activities.* These 15 activities involve students, parents, and school staff in building a caring, inclusive school environment. Such activities as Welcoming Newcomers, Grandpersons Gathering, Family Heritage Museum, and Schoolwide Mural Painting are detailed in the book *At Home in Our Schools* (Child Development Project, 1994), along with the materials and procedures needed to implement each one. Also described is a structure and process for involving diverse parents and school staff members in choosing, adapting, and staging the activities.

Over time, these approaches are intended to lead students to naturally reflect on the ways that they treat one another and on the feelings and perspectives of others. In addition to promoting academic motivation and learning, they are designed to help students understand one another, build social bonds, internalize the fundamental values that underlie our democratic society, and become intrinsically motivated to act on those values.

THE EFFECTS OF CDP AND COMMUNITY BUILDING

A large-scale comparative evaluation of CDP was conducted from 1991 to 1996. The study involved 12 CDP program schools and 12 matched comparison schools in six school districts nationally. These districts ranged in character from large and urban to small and rural. The major results from this evaluation demonstrated (a) the importance of building community in school for students' overall development and (b) the CDP's effectiveness at building sense of community when it was well implemented (Battistich, Watson, Solomon, Lewis, & Schaps, 1999; Schaps, Watson, & Lewis, 1996; Watson, Battistich, & Solomon, 1997).

The evaluation showed that implementation of CDP was substantial in 5 of the 12 program schools and weak in the remaining 7 schools. In the five "high-implementing" schools, teacher practices changed significantly in line with the CDP's principles and methods, relative to teacher practices in the matched comparison schools.

During 4 years of annual assessments, students in the five high-implementing schools, relative to their comparison school counterparts, showed significantly greater

- Concern for others
- Altruistic behavior
- Motivation to be kind and helpful
- Conflict resolution skill
- Acceptance of outgroups
- Enjoyment of class
- Liking for school
- Motivation to learn
- Time spent reading
- Resistance to use of alcohol or marijuana

Students in the five high-implementing CDP schools also showed significantly stronger sense of community as measured by a 31-item questionnaire scale that taps both perceptions of a supportive, friendly environment (e.g., "People in this school care about each other," "Students in this school help each other, even if they are not friends") and of influence or "voice" at school (e.g., "The teacher and students decide together what the rules will be" and "Students have a say in deciding what goes on"). Further analyses (Solomon, Battistich, Watson, & Schaps, 2000) showed that this bolstering of sense of community mediated all of the positive student outcomes just listed (Battistich & Hom, 1997; Battistich, Schaps, Watson, Solomon, & Lewis, 2000; Solomon, Battistich, Watson, Schaps, Lewis, 2000), as well as a number of additional positive outcomes (e.g., trust in teachers, self-esteem, sense of efficacy). In other words, CDP's broad-ranging impact was in large part due to its effectiveness at building community in school.

In a follow-up study involving three of the six districts, students from high-implementing CDP schools continued to out-perform comparison students during the middle school years. During middle school, former CDP students had significantly higher

- Involvement in positive group activities such as school sports, other extracurricular activities, and community youth groups
- Educational aspirations and expectations
- Trust in and respect for teachers
- Liking for school
- Grades
- Achievement test scores

Also, former CDP students were less likely to disobey school rules, cheat on a test, show disrespect for teachers, skip school without an excuse, or engage in serious delinquent acts such as carrying a weapon, using a weapon in a fight, selling drugs, or committing burglary.

Why does fostering a sense of community in school have such broad and lasting effects? When educators meet students' basic needs for close, caring relationships and a sense of influence and contribution, they help their students become committed to the school's values and goals. Students strive to fit in and to succeed in such schools, just as they try to emulate parents to whom they feel close. When a school engenders a sense of community, peer group dynamics tend to work in support of, rather than contrary to, its goals and values, thereby increasing the likelihood of positive effects.

PROGRAM ADOPTION

Because of the CDP's demonstrated effects, the U.S. Department of Education has listed it as an effective violence prevention program as well as an "Obey-Porter" (Comprehensive School Reform Demonstration) model, and the U.S. Center for Substance Abuse Prevention has selected it as a model drug prevention program. The CDP has also been cited as exemplary by the National

Association of Elementary School Principals, National School Board Association, Character Education Partnership, and National Council for Social Studies.

Because of its broad scope and complexity, the original CDP program was challenging to implement. Consequently, the Developmental Studies Center recently revised CDP to strengthen its focus, increase its feasibility, and decrease its cost of adoption. As now constituted, the emphasis is on four of its original components: its class meetings, buddies, parent involvement, and schoolwide components. The intent is to focus tightly on strengthening community, using the components that are most practical, affordable, and directly targeted at this goal.

The streamlined approach also has been renamed the Caring School Community to better signal its goal of building community in school. It is also a signal to school administrators that it is not a discrete, isolated program but rather an approach to schoolwide change designed to help produce students whose strengths in academics and character will be sources of pride to one's community and beyond. An independent multiyear evaluation of the revised procedures is currently underway, and its "early returns" are quite promising.

Caring School Community materials and staff development are available from the Developmental Studies Center. The materials consist of the books referenced earlier for its four components and videos that can be used for orientation and training purposes. On-site workshops are available to schools and districts, as are training-of-trainers institutes for school teams of 3 to 6 people, headed by a principal. The Developmental Studies Center can be reached at (800) 666-7270 or www.devstu.org.

Finally, other CDP-related materials can still be obtained from the Developmental Studies Center, including those for the literature-based reading, cooperative learning, and discipline approaches described earlier.

REFERENCES

Battistich, V., & Hom, A. (1997). The relationships between students' sense of their school as a community and their involvement in problem behaviors. *American Journal of Public Health, 87,* 1997–2001.

Battistich, V., Schaps, E., Watson, M., Solomon, D., & Lewis, C. (2000). Effects of the Child Development Project on students' drug use and other problem behaviors. *Journal of Primary Prevention, 21*, 75–99.

Battistich, V., Watson, M., Solomon, D., Lewis, C., & Schaps, E. (1999). Beyond the three R's: A broader agenda for school reform. *Elementary School Journal, 99*, 415–431.

Child Development Project. (1994). *At home in our schools: A guide to schoolwide activities that build community.* Oakland, CA: Developmental Studies Center.

Child Development Project. (1996). *Ways we want our class to be.* Oakland, CA: Developmental Studies Center

Child Development Project. (1997). *Blueprints for a collaborative classroom.* Oakland, CA: Developmental Studies Center.

Child Development Project. (2001). *That's my buddy.* Oakland, CA: Developmental Studies Center.

Dalton, J., & Watson, M. S. (1997). *Among friends: Classrooms where caring and learning prevail.* Oakland, CA: Developmental Studies Center

Kohn, A. (1990, January). The ABC's of caring. *Teacher Magazine,* 52–58.

Resnick, M. D., Bearman, P. S., Blum, R. W., Bauman, K. E., Harris, K. M., Jones, J., Tabor, J., Beuhring, T., Sieving, R. E., Shew, M., Ireland, M., Bearinger, L. H., & Udry, J. R. (1997). Protecting adolescents from harm: Findings from the national longitudinal study on adolescent health. *Journal of the American Medical Association, 278*, 823–832.

Schaps, E., Watson, M., & Lewis, C. (1996). A sense of community is key to effectiveness in fostering character education. *Journal of Staff Development, 17*, 42–47.

Solomon, D., Battistich, V., Watson, M., Schaps, E., & Lewis, C. (2000). A six-district study of educational change: Direct and mediated effects of the Child Development Project. *Social Psychology of Education, 4*, 3–51.

Watson, M. S. (2002). *Mrs. Ecken, Do You Like Me? Building Nurturing Relationships with Other People's Children.* Oakland, CA: Developmental Studies Center.

Watson, M. S., Battistich, V., & Solomon, S. (1997). Enhancing students' social and ethical development in schools: An intervention program and its effects. *International Journal of Educational Research, 27*, 571–586.

CHAPTER NINE

Educating for Social, Emotional, and Academic Development

The Comer School Development Program

Norris M. Haynes

What accounts for disparities in achievement and school adjustment among students, and especially between students in urban inner-city schools and those in more affluent suburban school districts? Social and school context factors appear to contribute more to a variance in school performance than personal and ability factors (Brookover, 1979). Rutter et al. (1977) noted that "schools comprise one facet in a set of ecological interactions and are subject to constraints by numerous social forces they cannot control." Yet they note that schools have considerable influence on the academic performance and life chances of students.

Sometimes the educator's view of the student's world is totally different from the student's view of his or her own world. Some educators see students in isolation from the rest of their phenomenological world and become constrained in their teaching of and interactions with many students by their narrow focus on the perceived limitations of these students. The challenges and opportunities offered by the urban environment and the positive attributes of the urban learner are often missed or simply ignored. This reduces the effectiveness of these educators and increases the risk of failure among students.

As a social organization, the school develops a culture of its own with norms and standards of behavior. Problems arise when conflicting norms, values, and standards evolve, or are brought into the school by subgroups, and there is cultural insensitivity, discrimination, and intolerance by educators. A cohesive climate in which everyone is respected is the basis for trust, full participation, and meaningful involvement. The evidence shows that a supportive, caring, culturally sensitive, and challenging school climate is a significant factor in the degree of school success experienced by urban students.

THE COMER SCHOOL DEVELOPMENT PROGRAM

The Comer School Development Program (SDP) was developed in response to the issues and opportunities present in urban schools at the time of its origin: poor school adjustment and low academic achievement among students in troubled schools. Comer's initial and continuing work attempts to create learning environments that respond to the developmental needs of students in a holistic way. The SDP incorporates and reflects several theoretical perspectives, including the population adjustment and social action perspectives (Reiff, 1966). The SDP resembles a social action model in that it attempts to serve children through social and educational change.

Comer has noted that because of experiences in families under stress during the preschool years, a disproportionate number of working-class and low-income children may present themselves to the schools in ways that are viewed and misperceived as "bad," showing a lack of motivation and demonstrating low academic potential. In reality, the undesirable and troubling behaviors often indicate inadequate development along any one or more of six critical pathways, to be discussed shortly. Undergirding the SDP is the belief that children who are developing well can learn adequately. Comer believes that positive interactions with meaningful authority figures—parents, teachers, administrators—who support child development simultaneously promote learning; furthermore, reasonable continuity of such relationships is needed.

Critical Developmental Pathways

At the core of the SDP is a focus on holistic child development along six interlocking pathways: physical, linguistic, ethical, social, psychological, and cognitive (Figure 9.1).

Physical

This pathway is concerned with promoting children's physical health. It includes good nutritional education and programs, physical health education and activities, and access to health and dental care education and services. Within this pathway, we also ensure that children's vision and hearing are checked as regularly as needed to ensure that they can see to read and hear well enough to learn and to understand subject matter content.

Linguistic

This pathway is concerned with helping children develop appropriate written and spoken language skills. An essential aspect of children's being healthy and maintaining their good physical and psychological health is the ability to articulate their needs, express their points of view, and engage in meaningful and

Figure 9.1   The Nine Component School Development Program: Three
                   Principles, Three Teams, and Three Operations.

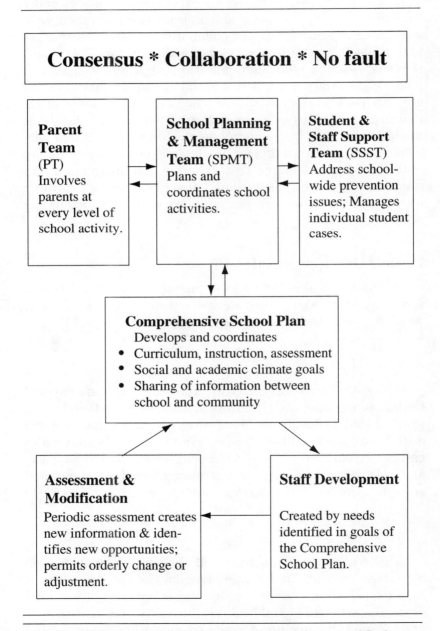

Consensus * Collaboration * No fault

Parent Team (PT)
Involves parents at every level of school activity.

School Planning & Management Team (SPMT)
Plans and coordinates school activities.

Student & Staff Support Team (SSST)
Address school-wide prevention issues; Manages individual student cases.

Comprehensive School Plan
Develops and coordinates
- Curriculum, instruction, assessment
- Social and academic climate goals
- Sharing of information between school and community

Assessment & Modification
Periodic assessment creates new information & identifies new opportunities; permits orderly change or adjustment.

Staff Development

Created by needs identified in goals of the Comprehensive School Plan.

Child & Adolescent Growth along the Six Developmental Pathways constructive conversation with others. Success in school and in life to a large extent depends on one's ability to communicate effectively through the written and spoken word.

Ethical

This pathway is concerned with helping children develop good decision-making skills. This involves helping them learn to make good judgments, especially in problem situations, and to make choices that are healthy and positive. Making wise choices in school and outside of school can make the difference between success and failure, health and illness, life and death. We must give children the skills to analyze and assess choice alternatives and decide on the best and most healthy choices. Good development along this pathway reduces the occurrence of high-risk behaviors such as alcohol and drug abuse, promiscuous and unprotected sexual activity (which can lead to early and unplanned pregnancies and sexually transmitted diseases, including AIDS), and reckless disregard for the rights of others.

Social

This pathway is concerned with promoting children's ability to interact socially with other children and with the significant adults in their lives. It has to do with what Howard Gardner called "interpersonal intelligence." The ability to problem solve in social situations and to negotiate constructively leading to win–win situations, reduces the incidence of violence in our schools and communities, and makes young people—and all of us—safer and more secure.

Psychological

This pathway is concerned with the intrapsychic well-being of children, their self-esteem, and their evaluations of their own worth and value as individuals—both in and outside of school. We must provide children in schools with experiences that lead to enhanced self-worth, self-efficacy, and well-being. We must also attend to the increasing incidence of depression and anxiety, and to the devastating impact of posttraumatic stress disorder (PTSD) resulting from exposure to violence, on children's psychological and emotional health.

Cognitive

This pathway focuses on providing children with the knowledge and skills that would enable them to think critically and to be creative. We must help children in schools acquire effective problem-solving skills and the ability to apply concepts of learning in a variety of contexts. When children develop well cognitively, they are likely to succeed in school and to lead productive and healthy lives as adults.

In the Comer SDP, schools help children to develop well along these six pathways by fostering collaboration between parents and staff, among school-based health and mental health providers, and by connecting health care providers and services to the school and to one another. A basic premise of the Comer SDP is that all children have the potential to succeed in school and in life, and that the realization of this potential depends on how well educators, families, communities, and educators work together to create environments that support child development; children who are developing well can learn adequately. Thus the creation of a positive school climate that nurtures and sustains good psychosocial development and high levels of academic performance is of central importance to the SDP. The SDP is driven by the notion that when adults support and nurture children effectively, children develop well along each of the six critical interlocking pathways. Failure to develop well along one or more of the pathways may have significant consequences for children's social and emotional health and for their academic performance.

Comer identified the need for staff training and preparation in child development and ecological systems understanding (Haynes, 1994). He asserted that many school staffs lack training in child development and behavior management and understand school achievement solely as a function of genetically determined intellectual ability and individual motivation. They may also lack the preparation needed to help underdeveloped children gain proficiency in the basic academic and social skills. Because of this, some schools are ill prepared to modify behavior or to close the developmental and academic gaps of their students. School staff members too often respond with punishment and low expectations. Such responses usually lead to more difficult staff–student interactions and, in turn, to difficult staff–parent and community interactions, staff frustration, and a still lower level of performance by students, parents, and staff. This cycle, most common in our urban schools, must be broken.

The SDP Components

Working collaboratively with parents and staff, the Comer team gradually developed a nine-component framework: three mechanisms, three operations, and three guidelines. The *three mechanisms* are (1) a school planning management team (SPMT) representative of the parents, teacher, administrators, and support staff; (2) a student and staff support team (SSST), which includes professional staff with child development and mental health knowledge, including school counselors, psychologists, social workers, special education teachers, a school nurse, and others; and (3) a parent program that involves parents at all levels of school life, including participation with staff on appropriate decision-making teams. The SPMT carries out *three critical operations:* the development of (1) a Comprehensive School Improvement Plan with specific goals in the social climate and academic areas; (2) staff development activities based on building level goals in these areas; and (3) periodic assessment that allows the staff to adjust the program to meet identified needs and opportunities.

Three essential guidelines and agreements are needed: (1) Participants on the SPMT cannot paralyze the principal, and the principal cannot disregard the input of the SPMT; (2) decisions are made by consensus to avoid "winner–loser" feelings and behavior; (3) a "no-fault," problem-solving approach is used by all of the working groups in the school. Eventually, these guidelines and associated attitudes permeate the organizational culture of the school and transform it into a learning community where child-centered education and learning takes place and sensitivity to child development undergirds all decisions that are made.

EXAMPLE FROM MEYERS PARK HIGH SCHOOL

Following is a case study analysis of the implementation of the SDP at Meyers Park High School, in North Carolina. Michael Ben-Avie, a member of the SDP research and evaluation staff, documented the way the comprehensive School Improvement Plan was developed by the school's SPMT. According to Ben-Avie (1998, pp. 64–65), the principal at Meyers Park noted the following:

> The Comer process allowed the teachers to have owner-ship of what was going on in the school. The Comprehensive School Improvement Plan was previously designed by four or five teachers when you're talking about 120 certified staff members at the school and a group of parents, as well as two students. When it was done last year, I took it through the Comer process. I sent a copy of the old plan to all of the committees. We're going to revise, we're going to come up with our plan for next year, I said. Give input, change, modify. I sent a copy of the whole old plan to every committee with a memo that asked them to give input to the whole plan and not only their specific area of interest. It was a total staff effort. Once the new plan began to develop, the committees would indicate the portion of the plan that they should be responsible for implementing. Every staff member served on a committee. During the planning process, they voiced issues and concerns that needed to be resolved or incorporated into the plan. While during the planning stage, they began to take ownership of strategies that needed to be implemented. Thus, it was a simultaneous process of discerning what the school needed and ensuring staff buy-in.
>
> I took a tentative plan to the Parent Committee. They gave suggestions, revisions, and so forth. I took the plan back to the staff. The School Planning and Management Team (SPMT) compiled all the input and came up with the new Comprehensive School Improvement Plan. Now, the plan is being implemented by everyone that's on the staff. In the past, there were complaints about the plan: What was it? What were we supposed to be doing? We voted on

the new plan in a faculty meeting and that was it. Now people know what they said needed to be done so they have ownership; they're doing it. They are turning in quarterly assessments to me so that I can see what strategies they are working on and implementing in their committees.

The story of how Meyers Park developed its Comprehensive School Improvement Plan does not end at this point, however. Just as the school finished its plan, a new superintendent came in and his three goals were literacy, safety, and community/parent involvement. The school went back to the plan. Every single department was able to add strategies that they would use to address these goals.

The Comprehensive School Improvement Plan is a 20-page document outlining goals, objectives, activities and strategies, necessary resources, time lines, responsible persons, and evidence of completion. Goals range from increasing communication between home and school to improving literacy. As the Comer process was implemented, the school community discussed strategies for increasing the enrollment of students placed at risk in the school's behavior improvement program. A department chair had been given an extra planning period to develop a support group to keep the at-risk students involved in the program and to work on recruitment. In the Comprehensive School Improvement Plan, goals aim to ensure that curriculum and instruction meet the full range of educational needs in serving a wide range of students. The objectives listed under this goal include using student data for planning, increasing the media center's support of the teaching–learning process, continuing to develop alternative programming to meet the diverse needs of students, and implementing special programs and courses to address the diversity of the student population.

At the January 7, 1997, SPMT meeting, the team discussed contacting parents of students who were at risk of failing. At the high school level, a student could have between six to eight teachers (and sometimes more if physical education and other activities were counted). A teacher, they decided, is to initiate contact with the student's guidance counselor via a form developed by the Research Committee. The guidance counselor has the perspective to see whether the student is in danger of failing only one class or several. The guidance counselor would notify the parents and talk with them about their child's overall progress at school.

The SPMT next met on January 23. The team discussed the importance of considering each other's feelings and avoiding "finger pointing" during meetings. They agreed to allot an approximate time for each topic on the agenda to avoid digressions, to make every effort to meet the following year during fifth period (instead of after school) when people tend to be more alert, and to keep in mind that they represent groups, not themselves personally. During the meeting, the team heard about the progress of the tutoring program. Thirty-five tutors had been trained. Teachers were asked to provide the tutors with adequate materials and detailed objectives to ensure the program's success. Staff and parents complimented the Comer committees for having done a great job in supplying hard-copy evidence that they had been implementing strategies to improve the school.

> In reflection on the SDP and the changes at Meyers Park, Lloyd Wimberley, a staff member observed: "a high school can be pulled in so many different directions at the same time. It's a very complex and very differentiated kind of organization. The SDP creates a common language. It creates a common view that is student-centered. This helps us get on the same page together and realize the common interests." (Ben-Avie, 1998, p. 65)

EFFECTS OF THE COMER SCHOOL DEVELOPMENT PROGRAM

The SDP has had multiple and significant effects on aspects of students' social, emotional, and academic development.

Analysis of data from studies in New York, New Haven, Chicago, and other school districts indicates significant program effects on student achievement. Many schools where the SDP has been implemented successfully experience significant student academic growth on standardized measures of achievement, including state criterion referenced tests and norm referenced tests

(Haynes, 1998). Data also indicate that school-related attitudes and behaviors are also positively affected. There have been significant decreases in absenteeism, suspensions, and referrals for disciplinary problems (Comer, Haynes, & Hamilton-Lee, 1988). Studies on SDP effects on social and emotional development showed that the program has had a positive effect on students' self-concept, feelings of efficacy, motivation to achieve, and their social competence (Becker & Hedges, 1992; Cauce, Comer, & Schwartz, 1987; Cook, 1998; Haynes, 1994; Haynes & Comer, 1990, 1993).

Policy Implications

The work in the SDP has significant implications for the reformulation of national education and social policy and the refocusing of educational practice across the United States. Over the past decade, and recently with the national focus on systemic school reform, Comer and his colleagues have informed and in some cases led the debate about what true educational reform means and what it must entail. They have asserted time and time again that genuine reform in education must focus on addressing a number of key issues. These include the following:

1. *There should be greater focus on, and support given to, preschool readiness programs and early childhood education.* The evidence is clear that urban students in particular lose considerable academic ground even before they set foot in kindergarten. This, plus what is known about brain development in early childhood, places a premium on early education and care.

2. *Schools must be made an important and integral service component of the community.* The mission of the school changes from being only the purveyor of knowledge to being a central coalescing agent in which vital services for children and families are provided in an integrated way. The relationship between learning and socioeconomic development is clearly recognized, and the school's action plan reflects this awareness. The Comprehensive School Improvement Plans in all of the SDP schools include goals that address the relationship between the school and community. Activities are designed that promote an interface between service and school programs. Thus, the school becomes a true member of the community.

3. *Schools should be reorganized from hierarchical management systems of governance to systems of collaboration and involving all key stakeholders in children's education.* This requires that the power to make decisions and to establish policy should not be the domain of any one individual or group of individuals but be shared among school administrators, staff, and parents who work in mutually respectful, supportive, and rewarding ways, guided by considerations of which decisions are best for children.

4. *Access to family services in school communities should be increased.* This would allow parents and children to have basic physical and psychological needs met with minimum difficulty. We should not expect families to access community-based services, particularly when the complexities of managed care are involved. Increasing the presence of family services in schools leads to greater utilization and more preventive use of services.

5. *School curricula and the social developmental experiences of children should be infused with the notions of self-respect and of respect for others.* This involves promoting responsible behavior and values that are consistent with good citizenship and exemplary lives. There can be no distinction between the character of students and what they learn academically and interpersonally. Therefore, an explicit emphasis must be made on promoting responsible behavior and values consistent with exercising good citizenship and leading exemplary lives.

6. *Educators must recognize the centrality of the family in the child's learning and development, seeking meaningful ways to involve parents and guardians in schooling experiences.* Families and schools ought to be seen as partners, not as antagonists. Parents should not be seen as peripheral to the educational enterprise. This approach requires well-defined mechanisms and strategies for ensuring meaningful parent involvement, including flexible workplace policy adjustments that allow parents to participate more fully in their children's education.

7. *The system of educational assessment that relies too heavily on standardized norm referenced testing, which in many instances is biased and unfair to children and minorities, should be converted to a system that is more performance-based, diagnostic, and authentic.* This would be more consistent with a developmentally sound

educational approach. The SDP espouses and supports the use of alternative assessment strategies, such as portfolios and exhibitions of students' work, combined with more traditional forms of assessment. These methods allow for consistent and continuous insight into students' creative capacities and intellectual skills.

8.   *Sensitive and responsive curricula and pedagogical approaches should be developed.* These should acknowledge the diverse needs of children from various cultural, racial, ethnic, and socioeconomic groups, as well as children with varying degrees of physical, cognitive, or psychological needs.

9.   *Attention should be given to child development issues, the principles of which should be incorporated into inservices for practicing teachers.* For the most part, schools of education have failed to prepare teachers who are sufficiently knowledgeable about child development issues and sensitive to the influence of these issues on learning. It is important to modify and strengthen the curriculum and preservice practice experiences at colleges and universities to provide prospective teachers, administrators, and professional support staff (including school counselors, psychologists, and social workers) with a firm grounding in child development.

FINAL THOUGHTS

The evidence clearly suggests that when the Comer SDP is implemented well, it improves school and classroom climate and enhances students' academic and social behaviors (see Figure 9.2). The SDP is an effective process for improving schools. It is not a magic solution, but a commonsense approach to school reform that is grounded in sound child development principles. Our continuing documentation shows that significant positive effects on school and student performance outcomes are achieved with successful implementation of the Comer SDP. The growth trajectories among the lowest achieving schools that adopt, and consistently and faithfully implement, the Comer SDP support the view that a student-centered, developmentally sensitive approach works. Sustained change and commensurate positive student outcomes result from continuous dedication and renewal of commitment among all of the adults in children's lives. Such efforts

Figure 9.2   Effects of the Comer School Development Program.

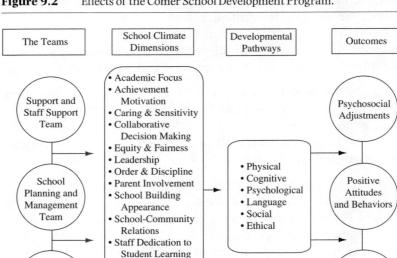

transform schools into caring, sensitive, and challenging learning and development communities.

REFERENCES

Becker, J. B., & Hedges, L. V. (1992). *A review of the literature on the effectiveness of Comer's School Development Program.* New York: Rockefeller Foundation.

Ben-Avie, M. (1998). The School Development Program at work in three high schools. In N. M. Haynes (Guest Ed.), Changing schools for changing times: The Comer School Development Program [Special issue]. *Journal of Education for Students Placed At Risk, 3*(1), 53–70.

Brookover, W. (1979). *School social systems and student achievement.* New York: Praeger.

Cauce, A. M., Comer, J. P., & Schwartz, D. (1987). Long-term effects of a systems oriented school prevention program. *American Journal of Orthopsychiatry, 57,* 127–131.

Comer, J. P., Haynes, N. M., & Hamilton-Lee, M. (1988). School power: A model for improving black achievement. *Urban League Review, 11,* 187–200.

Cook, T. (1998). Report on the Comer Process in Prince Georges County, Maryland.

Haynes, N. M. (1988). *School Development Program: Jackie Robinson Middle School follow-up study report.* New Haven, CT: Yale Child Study Center.

Haynes, N. M. (1994). *School Development Program SDP Research Monograph.* New Haven, CT: Yale University Child Study Center.

Haynes, N. M. (Guest Ed.). (1998). Changing schools for changing times: The Comer School Development Program [Special issue]. *Journal of Education for Students Placed At Risk, 3*(1).

Haynes, N. M., & Comer, J. P. (1990). The effects of a school development program on self-concept. *Yale Journal of Biology and Medicine, 63,* 275–283.

Haynes, N. M., & Comer, J. P. (1993). The Yale school development program: Process, outcomes and policy implications. *Urban Education, 28,* 166–199.

Haynes, N. M., Comer, J. P., & Hamilton-Lee, M. (1988). The school development program: A model for school improvement. *Journal of Negro Education,* 57(1), 11–21.

Reiff, J. (1966). Mental health manpower and institutional change. *American Psychologist, 21,* 540–548.

C H A P T E R   T E N

The Children's Institute Model for Building the Social–Emotional Skills of Students in Special Education

A Schoolwide Approach

Mindy Cohen

Bruce Ettinger

Therese O'Donnell

William, a 10-year-old boy who experienced intermittent rage disorder with attentional deficiencies and oppositional defiance, was accepted at The Children's Institute (TCI) midyear. His negative comments, aggressive and noncompliant behaviors would usually have a dramatic, deleterious impact on a classroom climate. The parties involved immediately scheduled a meeting that included the teacher, the school clinician, the problem-solving support team, and the consulting psychiatrist to develop a plan of action. Through the use of the TCI social problem-solving curriculum, classroom social–emotional skills groups, TCI's token economy, and individual cognitive–behavioral counseling, William's social competence increased. He practiced using problem-solving steps introduced in the classroom. He developed new coping strategies that addressed behavioral problems that occurred at home, with peers, and with staff. In addition, TCI's family education component promoted a home–school partnership as William's parents learned improved communication techniques and social problem-solving skills and self-esteem enhancement strategies to reinforce William's newly acquired skills at home and in the community. Not only was the staff pleased to observe William's social–emotional growth, but his parents also noticed positive changes in his self-esteem and overall happiness. All William knew was that he was excited when he made friends with two neighbors who previously would not play with him.

It is essential that schools develop comprehensive programs to promote the social–emotional learning of children in special education. In addition to having to overcome the negative social factors experienced by all children, their acquiring social–emotional skills is negatively impacted by the nature of their disabilities, including distractibility, impulsivity, visual and auditory deficits, language disorders, cognitive impairments, processing problems, and lack of mobility. Children with disabilities may find it difficult to learn important social cues, understand subtleties of language, express their feelings, perceive others' feelings accurately, and acquire problem-solving skills. Limited social experiences and skills impede success in academics, sports, and social relationships, thereby negatively affecting their self-esteem.

The TCI model has evolved in response to the unmet social–emotional needs of children exhibiting a wide range of learning and developmental difficulties. This approach has demonstrated the beneficial results of implementing a schoolwide, comprehensive, curriculum-based social–emotional learning program. Rather than providing counseling and other related services within a vacuum, the TCI model is delivered within the context of an overall social–emotional skills development paradigm.

BACKGROUND

The Children's Institute (TCI), a New Jersey State Board of Education–approved, private special education school for students who exhibit behavioral, emotional, and learning disabilities; pervasive developmental delays; and autism, was the fertile ground in which Dr. Bruce Ettinger, TCI's executive director/superintendent, cultivated and nurtured the TCI model. Dr. Ettinger understood that students' deficits in social–emotional skill development must be met with a powerful, positive, integrated educational response that addressed these difficulties and their unique learning, cognitive, and language skills needs.

Changing Nature of Services to Children

Over the past two decades, many educators believed that behavior modification was the best solution for "managing" the social, emotional, and behavioral problems found in the school setting. TCI was convinced early on that this method, which still exists in many educational settings, was insufficient because behavior modification alone could not supply the "glue" needed to tie together a comprehensive, schoolwide approach. TCI embraced social–emotional skill training developed in the 1970s as an additional (fourth) approach, complementing the three major psychological approaches used to alter the behavior of emotionally disabled children and to promote their social–emotional well-being: (a) psychodynamic, (b) humanistic–nondirective, and (c) behavior modification. Social–emotional skills training is different from approaches that rely on interventions such as interpretations, reflective listening, or reinforcement to unlock the appropriate prosocial skills assumed to exist with the child but that are not being expressed or used. Most important, social–emotional skills training provides an approach to viewing the behaviorally disabled child in educational and pedagogic terms, rather than clinical terms. The instructor assumes the emotionally disabled child lacks or is weak in certain social–emotional skills and is in need of being taught behaviors essential for life success.

Changing the Configuration of Services

The Peacock Hill Working Group stated in 1991 that "the current state of affairs does not indicate a lack of knowledge and effective interventions and approaches, but a lack of commitment, advocacy, and scarcity of resources that stymie their implementation" (p. 301). Studies also show that most mental health professionals usually do not receive the necessary training to collaborate adequately with school personnel in providing essential support and consultative services. As the need for expanded educational services continued to grow, the U.S. Department of Education indicated in the Tenth Annual Report to Congress in 1998 that there is a dramatic shortage of teachers prepared to instruct pupils with emotional disabilities.

Since 1989, The Children's Institute acknowledged that reliance on a pullout mental health program, inadequate collaboration with mental health providers, behavioral programs emphasizing classroom management rather than affective education and social skill development, limited staff development, and isolated parent support and education resulted in unacceptable practices. An effective program to meet the increasingly serious difficulties of students must be integrated within all aspects of the special educational setting throughout the entire school day. Furthermore, the work of Dr. James Comer provided inspiration that a truly far-reaching social development and learning approach must transcend the school. Therefore, the TCI model is built on the understanding that social and emotional development must be transferred from the school to the family and the community.

Special education schools serving students with serious emotional disorders that adversely affect educational performance and functioning are forced to accommodate youngsters with more severe behavioral issues. This is further complicated because medical insurance coverage demands shortened psychiatric hospitalizations, referrals to residential settings are few and far between, and aggressive violent behavior in children and adolescents is dramatically increasing. At the same time that special education laws and the Individuals with Disabilities Education Act's discipline code for disability-related behaviors have limited out-of-school suspensions and expulsions, requiring development of alternative educational programs, mainstream education programs have adopted a "zero tolerance" policy toward children who demonstrate behavioral disturbances and discipline problems. For these reasons, the TCI model helps schools serving this student population to meet these challenging needs.

THE TCI MODEL

Through cycles of design, implementation, and feedback, the TCI model has evolved to become increasingly effective in anticipating and responding to the challenges of educating students with serious emotional disabilities. In 1989, TCI discovered Social Decision Making (Elias & Clabby, 1989), a comprehensive social problem solving (SPS) curriculum that integrates many of the essential components that can be adapted for social–emotional skills training for students with more severe emotional disorders (SEDs). TCI uses a cognitive–behavioral approach with all students, ranging from those with cognitive or language weaknesses (or both) to higher functioning students. This involves a step-by-step process to teach students what they need to do to develop socially appropriate replacement behaviors. On a regular basis, students also participate in "practice and rehearsal" of skills specific to the needs of the individual child. It is through this technique that students learn to replace inappropriate actions with appropriate ones within a specific situation. This method is based on the extensive works of Dr. Maurice Elias (Elias & Tobias, 1996), Dr. Arnold Goldstein's *Skillstreaming* curriculum (McGinnis & Goldstein, 1984), and Dr. Frank Gresham's *Social Skills Intervention Guide* (Elliott & Gresham, 1992). These works focus on the social and emotional learning of all children; using the cycle of design, implementation, and feedback for more than a decade, TCI staff members revised—and continue to revise today—the works to reflect the unique needs of our students. We then added lessons promoting self-esteem and other social–emotional skills. This evolved into TCI's Social Development Curriculum.

The TCI model incorporates the common vocabulary found in Elias and Clabby's (1989) approach. A 1989 pilot program introduced the SPS vocabulary to all students and staff members, including administrators, teachers, assistants, "specials" (such as art, music, physical education, and computer teachers), clinicians, problem-solving counselors, and TCI's consulting psychologist and psychiatrist. The use of this shared language created far greater continuity in care for the students than had previously been in evidence. Messages to them about their behavior, learning, and communication were clearer, less confusing, and more efficiently understood.

It is this commitment to a schoolwide approach that has been the hallmark of our work at TCI and what we believe to be the essential element in our success. Meeting the educational needs of our most challenged students requires educational leaders to take on the greatest challenges. We have found, however, that doing so also yields great rewards. In the following section, we illustrate all of the components that we work to put in alignment so that others may replicate our process.

TCI'S SCHOOLWIDE APPROACH TO SOCIAL LEARNING

Social–Emotional Learning Skills: A Curriculum-Based Approach

Cathy is an eight-year-old elective mute who participated for months in the classroom Sharing Circle. She was physically present but did not use any verbal language. She would, however, appropriately accept the "Speaker Power" object and pass it to her classmate. She indicated her listening skills through gestures or written responses. After four months of exposure to this aspect of social problem solving, she delighted her teachers and classmates by responding with a verbal "yes or no" response. This eventually led to Cathy using short sentences.

Working with children like Cathy and others at TCI requires that they develop skills for living, and these skills are imparted through a curriculum structure that pervades the entire school. Staff members relate to this structure and the social–emotional skills it develops, regardless of whether they actually teach the skills. Before describing different staff roles in the school, an overview of some key skills and how they are conveyed in the curriculum follows.

A "Sharing Circle" provides an opportunity for students to develop many attitudes that build group cohesiveness and class unity. Students gain respect for differences of opinions while developing trust through sharing their thoughts and feelings. The goal is not to put students on the spot, but to provide an opportunity to speak and be listened to without interruption. Listening is a critical skill for learning and for getting along with others. Success in life depends in part on one's ability to participate in groups and listen to other people's points of view. Knowing when to listen, when to talk, and how to develop and connect ideas that different people in the group express are important social development skills.

Another tool that children enjoy using is called "Speaker Power." This technique allows students to practice taking turns and can help them remember to listen and pay attention to the person who is speaking. Teachers use items that are appropriate at various levels, such as a stuffed animal for grades K–3 and a koosh ball for middle and upper grades.

Listening, one of the first readiness skills taught, is especially challenging for impulsive children to learn. Although critical to the development of social competence and self-esteem in all children, TCI students often lack this skill, so necessary for building friendships and being included in play situations. The TCI model teaches students the basics of "Listening Position" in a fun and playful way. For example, a photograph of a staff member is taken to demonstrate poor "Listening Position," and another is taken to show good Listening Position. The students enjoy seeing the funny pictures of teachers, and these easily created teaching aids can be used to decorate the classroom. Students also have an opportunity to demonstrate the difference between what Listening Position is and what it is not as they practice this skill and receive positive encouragement. In addition, students have made Listening Position books. Using a Polaroid camera, students pose in proper Listening Positions in all areas of the building—classroom, art room, music room, lunch room, and so on. The book is used as a visual prompt to gently remind students of proper Listening Positions when he or she may be experiencing difficulty with this skill.

Conrad, a quiet child with an attention-deficit/hyperactivity disorder classification, had a very low frustration tolerance. When we found his frustration building, his anger would often erupt like a volcano. We worked to help him identify his Feelings Fingerprints before the outburst, and then the teacher or problem-solving counselors practiced the Keep Calm breathing exercises. After a period of weeks, he would automatically begin using the breathing exercises in crisis situations. This made him more approachable and available to brainstorm more appropriate alternatives when he perceived himself to be in a vulnerable situation.

Many problem behaviors in children are preceded by their experiencing "Feelings Fingerprints" (their body's characteristic way or ways of letting them know when they are under stress, such as a stomachache, clenched fists, rapid heartbeat, tightness in the chest). Feelings Fingerprints are the first sign of what can become much stronger emotional reactions in children with serious emotional disorders. Emotions or feelings exacerbated by an underlying psychiatric condition can flood the brain's pathways for clear thinking and make it difficult to handle upsetting social situations. The TCI model recognizes the importance of helping children to master the way they think and act when an upsetting incident happens and to do so at the earliest possible time.

Students also learn how to use important skills such as being able to calm down, think clearly, and present themselves appropriately in social situations. TCI students learn to identify "trigger situations," so that they know which circumstances lead them to "lose their cool" and experience strong emotions that they find difficult to regulate. Although anyone can lose self-control in a trigger situation, this is even more challenging for children with serious emotional or behavioral problems because of poor impulse control.

Once students are aware of what causes them to become upset, they begin to slowly develop the skills needed to stay in control. "Keep Calm" is a technique that involves self-talk, controlled breathing, and imagery to help children stop and think more clearly before acting (Elias & Tobias, 1996). Once TCI students have learned to Keep Calm in stressful situations, they are challenged to begin learning to communicate their feelings and intentions assertively.

B-E-S-T is introduced to TCI students in creative ways to compensate for language-based deficits. Students internalize an effective communication style as they learn to appropriately express themselves through Body language (B), Eye contact (E), Speech (S), and Tone of voice (T). Students with more severe difficulties benefit from frequent reinforcement so that they remember to pay attention to the style of communication used in social interactions, because this is critical in establishing positive relationships. With creative lessons and lots of practice, support, and patience, students can feel calmer, more under control, and more capable of dealing with the stressful situation.

Staff Orientation

Extensive staff development and ongoing support continue to be the hallmark of this model. In August, the supervisor of instruction and the social development coordinator (see section on this position below) invite new staff members to an orientation and training session. After a brief explanation of the program's history, participants begin to conceptualize the rationale for the schoolwide integration of social emotional development. This reinforces the significant role that every staff member contributes to the overall program success. Professional development for new and experienced staff is ongoing throughout the school year.

Because most of TCI's social development classroom lessons begin with a "Sharing Circle," the supervisor of instruction and the social development coordinator next simulate a Sharing Circle as a way of "Getting to Know You" and as experiential practice. "Processing" the Sharing Circle reinforces some of the key concepts of an open group forum for exchanging ideas and solving problems while allowing group members the freedom to pass if they do not wish to contribute to the discussion. Sample Sharing Circle ideas are presented so new staff members can begin to create topics relevant for their students' needs and interests. It is recommended that Sharing Circle content move from unemotional to more personal topics and problems, from hypothetical to real, exactly as one would do with students.

TCI Curriculum Guides are reviewed by introducing the three-dimensional model derived from structured learning theory—"Discuss, Demonstrate, and Do"—to familiarize the new staff with readiness skills, common language terms, teaching techniques, and academic applications at the elementary and middle school levels. Staff members learn three broad skill areas that comprise the curriculum.

1. Self-control skills (learning to listen carefully and accurately and learning the Listening Position, remembering and following directions, Keep Calm before problem solving, starting a conversation and keeping it going, resisting provocations and keeping control)

2. Social awareness and group participation skills (Sharing Circle, teaching children how to role-play, developing and maintaining friendships, and asking for help)

3. Improving social decision-making and social problem-solving skills (introducing social problem-solving lessons, reviewing the problem-solving steps, looking for signs of different feelings in self and others, conflict resolution, and peer mediation)

For example, elementary teachers are expected to introduce the Sharing Circle, Keep Calm, Feelings Fingerprints, Friendship and Team-Building skills, and a basic overview of the Eight Steps to Social Problem Solving. For the first half of the year, the middle school program reinforces previously learned readiness skills (Team Building, Coping and Hassles, Asking and Giving Help, Dealing with Criticism, Values and Ethics, and Self-Esteem) before focusing on the eight-step model for the second half of the year. From year to year, this plan is modified and refined so as to meet most efficiently and effectively the needs of TCI students. The sequence of social skills taught varies.

Schoolwide Skill Reinforcement

At the elementary and middle school levels, specific social development skills are introduced or reinforced on a quarterly basis throughout the school. In the first quarter, elementary students learn about the Sharing Circle, Listening Position, and listening skills, whereas middle school students learn listening skills, following directions, and Keep Calm. During the second quarter, lower elementary grade students learn about following directions, Keep Calm, friendship, and conversation skills, whereas upper elementary students learn about resisting peer pressure, friendship, and conversation skills. Middle school students are introduced to the Eight Steps of Problem Solving, friendship, and conversation skills before conflict resolution, peer mediation, and feelings, and more about the "Eight Steps" skills are introduced in the third quarter. At the same time, elementary students continue to learn more about feelings, friendship, and an introduction to the Eight Steps. In June, all students practice role-playing scenarios to strengthen the skills taught throughout the year. From experience, staff members have learned the importance of going slower in the instruction of individual social skills, breaking them down into steps, and providing students more opportunities for practice and rehearsal.

Later on during the orientation, the entire staff joins in to share successful experiences and the ways in which SPS and social–emotional skill strategies were used to provide student opportunities to practice the essential life skills of listening, remembering, and thinking. The "seasoned" staff members also share techniques used to introduce other important readiness skills such as being able to calm down, think clearly, and present oneself appropriately in social situations. To enhance professional development (and students' opportunities to practice social–emotional skills), we also use videoconferencing, providing our staff and students with the opportunity to exchange ideas and collaboratively work with other schools.

The Social Development Coordinator

The role of the social development coordinator emerged from an identified need for an individual, within the school, to be responsible for the development and facilitation of program activities and the implementation of a schoolwide curriculum for their special needs students' social development. The coordinator receives a stipend or reduced schedule for chairing and planning monthly staff and social development committee meetings. The responsibilities and job description of the social development coordinator have evolved over the past few years. The position includes training new staff members during orientation; establishing the quarterly skills chart; developing the monthly staff meeting presentation schedule; providing workshop presentations to other special education schools; establishing additional subcommittees to address new ideas; ordering new materials; and locating new resources to maintain high program interest. As of the time of this writing, the position continues to evolve and change in accordance with TCI's needs. New clinical and instructional staff members have become involved in the process of curriculum development and training.

Monthly Staff Meetings

The quarterly Social Development Skills Chart identifies the schoolwide "Topic of the Month" so that the entire TCI staff works on similar skills at the same time and so that special subject teachers know which skills students are learning so they are able to reinforce the common terms throughout each subject taught. An organizational flow chart outlines a monthly schedule for teachers to share specific skill-based lessons with other staff members. They will demonstrate and make available to their colleagues creative props and supporting materials to supplement lessons from magazines, newspapers, and video-based vignettes. SPS posters, displayed in all of the classrooms, are also used in therapy, art, speech, music, and physical education. This coordinated effort to share successful lessons and materials at each class level has led to innovative thinking and creativity and has infused great energy into the teaching process.

Social Development Committee Meetings

Monthly Social Development Committee meetings scheduled with administrators, clinicians, and representatives from each division and specialty allow committee members to bring back information to their colleagues. In return, teachers share insights with their committee representative, who then brings the ideas to the next Social Development Committee meeting so that all aspects of the curriculum are fully integrated throughout the entire school. For example, an outgrowth of this process was the creation of the Social Decision-Making Chart that helps elementary-level students identify problems, good choices and poor choices, and corresponding consequences. Another example is the middle school Mood Diary, developed so that students learn about emotional regulation by recording and gauging their varying degrees of anger during a situation that triggers angry or other negative feelings. The corresponding elementary tool, the Feelings Thermometer, produces the same result as the Mood Diary but is more concrete and visual, especially for the younger student dealing with attention-deficit/hyperactivity disorder, obsessive–compulsive disorder, a pervasive developmental disorder, or emotional disabilities.

Schoolwide Crisis and Supplemental Problem-Solving Support Services

Supplemental problem-solving support services provide an integrated approach in which social problem-solving and social–emotional skills training function together. Problem-solving counselors and the Problem Solving Room are crucial elements of TCI's comprehensive initiative that have evolved since 1994. Before that time, students spent time in "detention" with a "crisis worker" so that the classroom teacher would be able to continue the lesson without disruption. Although this practice has limited demonstrated effectiveness, it still exists in many educational settings. TCI staff members realized that an approach emphasizing consequences could not change a disruptive behavior pattern because the process did not provide an opportunity for social–emotional learning to stop the negative cycle. What was needed was something that addressed the causes of a behavior problem exhibited in students as related to difficulties at home and with peers and staff members in the school.

As part of the clinical staff trained in crisis prevention, problem-solving counselors, who are social workers or certified psychologists, work with "referred" students when they are unable to calm down. The teacher first gives the student "sit and think" and problem-solving time in the classroom. If the student is unable to problem solve in the classroom, he or she may be asked to go to the Problem Solving Room, where counselors and students work through problem-solving steps to reinforce skills previously introduced in the classroom. This interaction provides an opportunity to practice and rehearse specific social–emotional skills. The counselor's primary goal is to support the teacher in providing students with the opportunity to develop coping strategies and insight into their actions. These techniques foster social competency and establish the essential groundwork for building social competence and appropriate social–emotional skill development in students with serious social, emotional, and behavioral deficits. We are impressed with the increasing number of children who request problem solving; furthermore, staff have noted that once students begin to verbalize their feelings and problem solve, there has been a decrease in aggressive and acting-out behaviors. In light of the increasing number of children admitted to TCI exhibiting aggressive and impulsive behaviors, the problem-solving staff has increased to four professionals.

The Role of the School Clinician

The full-time school clinician, either a school social worker or psychologist, serves an integral role in the overall therapeutic milieu. The clinician combines a cognitive–behavioral approach, classical behavioral principles (TCI's Token Economy), and psychodynamic techniques to promote social competence through social–emotional skills training and social problem solving. The major services provided by the school clinician include individual and paired therapies, issues-based group therapy, weekly classroom social–emotional skills groups, and crisis intervention. Besides these direct student services, the school clinician also works with students during recess duty and various school functions that provide other opportunities to teach children problem-solving and social–emotional skills.

In addition to collaborating with the problem solving counselors and all other staff, the school clinician also works closely with TCI's consulting psychiatrist and psychologist as a "case manager." The school clinician seeks and coordinates the input of outside professionals and Child Study Team members to maximize the comprehensive integration of the TCI model integration throughout the school day and from school to the community. The roles of parent educator and case manager reflect TCI's emphasis on helping students generalize to their home environment the skills they have learned at school.

Family Component

The TCI model recognizes that it is important for parents and the school staff to form a partnership to enhance the social–emotional development of children. It is not enough simply to teach social–emotional skills in the school environment. Newly acquired skills must be reinforced at home so that the social–emotional skills are generalized from the school to the home to the community. Therefore, it is essential that parents learn strategies to increase their child's social competence through the effective use of communication techniques, praise, problem-solving skills, social–emotional skills, and self-esteem enhancement situations.

The purpose of parent education is to provide parents with the knowledge and skills necessary to promote their children's success and to foster a positive parent–child relationship. Parents receive updates and a copy of each lesson so they can review the lesson at home and encourage their child to use the social–emotional skill within the family setting. They are encouraged to follow the "Discuss, Demonstrate, and Do" model used in the classroom to provide the consistency necessary for skill development. Parents can play a crucial role in supporting social–emotional learning by appropriately managing their own feelings and behaviors, modeling healthy social interactions, and "facilitating" the step-by-step process of social–emotional skill development. To facilitate parents acquiring these skills, staff members model these approaches and parents have the opportunity to practice and apply these approaches to their unique home settings. A series of consecutive workshops provides parents the opportunity to try these approaches and continue to receive staff support and make necessary revisions. TCI is in the process of building up educational resources for parents and staff in the areas of social development, including new books, CDs, and professional development opportunities. We plan to include such material on TCI's Web site.

Social–Emotional Development
Applied to Academics

Social–Emotional Development skills are easily inserted into TCI's educational curriculum. For each subject area, teachers have creatively and effectively incorporated problem-solving techniques and readiness skills. For instance, the Sharing Circle lends itself nicely as an opener to a third-grade science lesson. A typical question for a lesson on water conservation might be, "Tell the group something that water can be used for." Identifying feelings in others can be addressed through a Venn diagram when comparing characters in a novel. The Eight Steps of Problem Solving can be used in a discussion on any historical or current event. The various methods of inserting problem-solving skills in the academic areas are endless. Using such an approach validates the importance of the skills in everyday life for the students. The TCI staff has created lesson plans in all academic areas in which problem-solving skills are incorporated and emphasized. Teachers have shared their lesson plans at staff meetings and distributed them for use in other classrooms.

Applications for Children With Pervasive Developmental Delays (PDD) or Autism

Teachers and parents often ask if the social–emotional development program could be applied to our students with PDD or autism. When students are deficient in auditory and visual memory, in language comprehension and processing, or in reading social–emotional cues, they are at a disadvantage when it comes to problem solving, role-playing, and imagining. This is because they have not integrated or comprehended the events of routine situations. We believe, however, that with more direction in the form of verbal and physical prompting, scripted language rephrasing and the use of social stories, we can help our students improve their social understanding of events. Social stories (Gray, 1994) specifically help teachers and parents understand both the child's perception of an event while at the same time providing them with the "why" of a given situation.

We must teach our students to become good listeners so that they can connect with their social partners. The more astute we are in comprehending another person's viewpoint, the better listener and communicator we will become. A child's social–emotional skills or lack thereof has a definite correlation with his or her ability to use language functions effectively. Therefore, our social–emotional skills program for our PDD and autistic students begins with some of the most obvious functions, such as greeting, requesting, commenting, and responding. Children move on as they can to the more complete social development curriculum activities.

The lessons are taught in the morning and reviewed at the end of each day. There are group contingency reinforcers, as well as points earned throughout the day and displayed on a social–emotional skills chart in the classroom. TCI's social–emotional skills lessons for PDD and autistic students have improved students' use of pragmatic language; ultimately we hope they also will improve the ability among these students to determine probable causes of events and to predict outcomes of their actions. As educators, we recognize the importance of teaching our students to think for themselves and to reason logically in solving problems.

CONCLUSION: NEXT STEPS FOR THE READER

This brief chapter does not fully describe all aspects of the TCI model, which are now being prepared in book and curriculum forms. The inspiration of James Comer continually guides us; his collaborative model integrates the work of our school staff members, parents, and community leaders and empowers students while building their social and emotional skills. This work "raised the bar" for what one could expect of coordinated work in a regular education setting; the TCI model attempts to do the same for special education.

Although this may seem like it was a daunting process, TCI's commitment over the past decade provides the creative framework to generate momentum and excitement for the educational administrator who wants to adapt the TCI model or some of its components. Implementation research studies over the years have illuminated ways to improve the components, and outcome studies have shown that the impact has been positive. Over a decade of experience gained by The Children's Institute can provide the structure needed to support and generate excitement among administrators, staff members, parents, and the community. In light of all the negative messages and influences in today's media and on the Internet, and in the continuing shadow of terrorist attacks on mainland American soil, educators must meet the seriousness of the problems facing our students with a parallel response. Halfway measures will not produce lasting results. Students deserve and must be provided with the opportunity to develop social–emotional skills and competencies that can last a lifetime. This serves not only to benefit the children, but also creates a positive school climate shared by all; it is a beacon to the larger community. We must settle for nothing less.

AUTHOR'S NOTE

Important contributions to this chapter were made by Gina Catania, M.A., Supervisor of Instruction/Curriculum Coordinator; Tara Hayek, M.Ed., Supervisor of Instruction/Behaviorist; and Dr. Stuart Isralowitz, Clinical Coordinator/School Psychologist.

REFERENCES

Elias, M. J., & Clabby, J. F. (1989). *Social decision making: A curriculum guide for the elementary grades.* New Brunswick, NJ: Rutgers University Center for Applied Psychology.

Elias, M. J., & Tobias, S. E. (1996). *Social problem solving interventions in the schools.* New York: Guilford. (Available through www.nprinc.com)

Elliott, S., & Gresham, F. (1992). *Social skills intervention guide.* Circle Pines, MN: American Guidance Service.

Gray, C. (1994). *The new social story book.* Arlington, TX: Future Horizons.

McGinnis, E., & Goldstein, A. P. (1984). *Skillstreaming the elementary school child.* Champaign, IL: Research Press.

Peacock Hill Working Group. (1991). Problems and promises in special education and related services for children and youth with emotional or behavioral disorders. *Behavior Disorders, 16,* 299–313.

CHAPTER ELEVEN

Social–Emotional Learning at North Country School

Resourcefulness,
Ruggedness, and Resilience

Frank Wallace

LEARNING ABOUT THE CYCLES OF LIFE AND DEATH

Friendly, an 8-year-old mare, died yesterday of colic. The news finds its way to the school building and through the halls. The children talk, weep, embrace one another, and something resembling a primitive keening begins among the girls, even for those who have only a passing acquaintance with Friendly. The 9- and

10-year-old girls watch the older ones, matching their own faces as best they can to those they observe, waiting to be included in the general embrace. Most of the boys watch from a distance, respectful, curious.

Frank, the head of the school, is in the hall. Ahrielle and Angela approach. They ask if they can be excused from their next class to say good-bye to Friendly in the pasture. No, Frank replies, but gives them a hug and some words of reassurance that Friendly will be there after classes are over.

Ana approaches Frank during lunch. It would be a good idea, she thinks, for all 40 children to go to the barn after lunch, just to reassure themselves that the rest of the animals are safe, that things haven't changed. At the conclusion of lunch, Frank stands as he does every day and hears announcements from various students and faculty members. At the conclusion of these, he talks about Friendly, reminding students how much horses dislike confusion. Calm, deliberation, regularity are what horses like, he says. Ten-year-old Devin raises his hand. "And chickens do, too," he adds. Leo, who never allows adults to get away with anything, raises his hand. "And children, too." He smiles to show that he knows what is going on even if others don't. "Right, Frank?"

Frank shares the suggestions that students have made and the leaders of afternoon activities agree to allow a time for barn and pasture visits. He reminds them also that the next morning after breakfast is their weekly town meeting and that this will be a time for them to say good-bye to Friendly as a community.

The next morning students gather for town meeting. They sit in a circle of chairs. Frank opens the meeting and invites people to talk about Friendly. Larry, who oversees the farm, tells the students about colic and why Friendly died. Then he reads a letter a woman wrote to a farm journal about life and death on a farm. Children begin to tell of their experiences over the past several years with Friendly. Tom tells about having been kicked one afternoon while he was cleaning out Friendly's stall. Martha talks about trying to get Friendly to jump and how often she has fallen. Ken, a faculty member, talks about a sharp turn that Friendly once made on a trail ride; Friendly pitched Ken 13 feet through the air, he remembers. A new teacher wonders how Friendly got her name. Diego, looking across the room at one of his 15-year-old peers, expands the irony: "For the same reason that Angel got called Angel," he offers. The boy so named laughs, and others laugh with him. The mood becomes more relaxed. Now children tell of pets that have died. "Where does the life go?" Sean asks. Sean is 11 years old. "It goes back into the world," Maya says. "It's like compost, only it's spirit."

Kathy, who is 13, tells of a cousin her own age who committed suicide. Tom talks about his grandfather's death. Joe and Carrie talk about how, in divorce, you can lose people without their actually dying. Bert takes the occasion to let the community know that his father is in prison. Amanda says she is going to make a box that will be buried with Friendly, into which people can put things that they have written or pictures that they have drawn.

As conversation about Friendly comes to an end, Patrick, who is 9 years old, and Winona, who is 10, announce that there are four new piglets at the barn and that their class has just named them Breakfast, Lunch, Dinner, and Snack. The meeting ends, and people go off to their classes.

A COMMUNITY OF 42 STUDENTS AND 24 ADULTS

Social and emotional learning (SEL) has been a part of the program at North Country School for 60 years. As new times have presented new challenges in the raising and teaching of children, the school has modified its approach. It is significant, however, that many of the school's time-tested practices work as well today as they did 60 years ago.

North Country School was founded in 1938 as a small coeducational boarding school. Its campus is a 160-acre farm 2,100 feet above sea level in the Adirondack Mountains. The children, ranging in age from 8 to 15 years, live with their teachers in groups of 8 or 10 in five "houses." There are 24 adults who work directly with the students from day to day. There are daily chores that involve caring for the animals, gardens, and facilities. The curriculum is standard for middle schools and uses the natural resources of the environment as teaching aids. Children of color comprise 40% of the population. Students represent 12 states and 5 foreign countries. The school is financed through a combination of fees, endowment income, and gifts. Student's full-scale

Wechsler Intelligence Scale (children's version) scores follow a bell curve between 100 and 165. The school's "three Rs" are resourcefulness, ruggedness, and resilience.

What our children have most in common is that they are away from home at an age when most children are not. They usually are here because something is not right at home. The dynamics of the family or the community might be wrong, and the child has been unsuccessful. The problem may be a contentious divorce, a recombinant family, a new marriage, or a sibling issue. Perhaps both parents are working 14-hour days, or perhaps there is only one parent, and she wants more of a life for herself. Or the parents travel or have undertaken research on gorillas in Africa. The consequence of our social dynamic is that we have many children who feel they have been "sent away." They may fear that they are unloved—or not loved enough—and this fear may take the form of anger. Peers take on the roles of siblings. House parent/teachers are employed in the child's emotional dynamic as parents.

Superficially, the school appears to be a pastoral paradise, a place where Norman Rockwell children build tree forts and play on a Currier and Ives landscape. But life is much more complicated than that, and it is these complications that have put social and emotional learning at the head of the school's agenda throughout its history.

The people at the school speak of themselves as a community. The day-to-day purpose of its childrearing and child-teaching strategies is to maintain harmony within the community. A broader purpose is to inculcate in the children a set of behaviors, values, and beliefs that will distinguish them as citizens in the communities they enter after they leave us.

THE CODE OF CONDUCT AND BEHAVIORAL OUTCOMES

The school's Code of Conduct is posted in places around the building and includes the following statement:

> We value community at North Country School and feel that we all learn and grow best in the context of many

caring relationships. If you behave kindly, respectfully and gently, you will grow and learn and feel like you belong to a caring community that will continue to nurture and protect you. If you do anything to hurt yourself, another person or the larger community, you will probably feel that you are less connected to the community.

The faculty is intentional about being a community and builds its program backward from an agreed-on set of behavioral outcomes. An example of this is found in the school's embrace of ecological balance as a real and metaphoric value: We try to live companionably with the land and its other inhabitants. When the local beaver population exploded several years ago, creating a lake between the school and its ski hill, several town meetings were spent debating alternative responses. Attempts were made at coexistence, then at relocating the beavers. Conduits were put under dams, dams were regularly broken up. These attempts failed, the situation worsened, and the community had to act aggressively to overcome this overpopulation. Classes worked on this problem on and off for much of the year.

The goals that North Country School has for SEL are the same as those embraced by the readers of this essay. The techniques and structures that we employ are, in some cases, different, and the combination of practices is unique, as it is in any school. Following is a list of some strategies and programs that represent the school's commitment to SEL.

SEL STRATEGIES AND PROGRAMS

- *Sustaining community, friendships, and facilities.* The concept of sustainable agriculture is basic to our ethic. By extension, it applies to sustaining community, friendships, and facilities. Conflicts cannot be left to molder in a corner; they must be worked through so that new understanding can emerge. It is not unlike putting our leavings back into the soil so that new plants may grow and nourish us.
- *People first, things second.* We believe that children learn people first and things second. They learn social and humane purposes through seeing them modeled; they learn the love of an art

or an idea through its practitioner. We try to fill this place with adults who model ideas and practices that are worth learning. This may well be the most important thing we do.

- *Simplicity.* We limit exposure to popular culture and simplify life as much as we can. No television. Personal electronics are limited to a child's room.

- *Key Kids.* Children who show responsibility in a normally locked school area (e.g., the library, dark room, computer room) are identified as "Key Kids," and their names are placed on a list attached to the key for that room. The key hangs in the staff room. The child may request the key at any time from a teacher.

- *Chores.* The children take doing real-work chores for granted. Such chores include feeding animals, gardening, harvesting, cleaning rooms, setting tables, and washing dishes. Adults do their share. By looking after the place we live, the animals on whom we depend for food and recreation, the land where our crops grow, and the woods that provide maple syrup and the fuel to boil it, we express our willingness to be responsible stewards of our habitation. Taking care of the land and its denizens, we find, is good practice for taking care of one another. We imagine this would be true in any school.

- *Caregiving.* When a child is ill and spends the day in her room, her roommate brings up the meals. This is practice in taking care of another person.

- *Candy as "stash."* We do not allow candy except as provided by adults on special occasions. This is one of the school's oldest and most effective practices. Banning candy of course creates significant incentive for "black market" practices and other kinds of benign acting-out against authority. Candy is called "stash." Children caught with candy lose small privileges. In my 7 years at the school, I have not had to deal with more than a couple misbehaviors involving alcohol, tobacco, or drugs. Children are too busy thinking about candy.

- *Public put-ups.* A "put-ups" board occupies a public space at the school. Students add slips of paper expressing gratitude or admiration for other students or teachers. Teachers do the same.

- *Morning meetings.* Each student's day begins with a 30-minute class meeting modeled on Ruth Charney's "Responsive Classroom" curriculum.

- *Interactive journaling.* Students in Grades 7 to 9 spend time once a week in the computer lab engaged in interactive journaling.

This involves one-on-one conversation with the Life Skills teacher, the making and updating of an autobiographical "hypercard" stack, and goal setting in the social, emotional, physical, and cognitive contexts.

- *Daily Council.* Council occurs every day after lunch. At this time, we recognize children who have shown generosity to the community, personal courage, endurance, trustworthiness, or other traits of which we often speak in town meeting. (The *Heroes* aspect of this program is derived from *The Kids' Guide to Character,* published by Free Spirits Press.)

- *Community Council.* A Community Council serves as a student government. It takes program initiatives, hears requests or complaints from students, and is a liaison to the faculty meeting. Older children earn the privilege of becoming mentors for younger children.

- *Town Meeting.* The head of the school leads town meeting once a week for 40 minutes. He tries to work through an agenda of topics as circumstance provides the opportunity. A meeting early in the year will invite students and adults to say why they are here and what they want to get out of the year. A case of theft encourages conversation about social contract. We believe that schools must teach the notion of social contract, the nature of personal freedom, and the reciprocal responsibilities that it brings. Our community meetings every week are forums for defining and redefining our commonalities, our differences, and for giving individuals a sense of their place in a small society.

- *Staff room log.* Teachers maintain a staff room log in which they record noteworthy behaviors, interpersonal incidents, and newly acquired information on a child. Like all schools, we never have enough time to share information with one another. The log helps make up for this problem.

- *"The Book" in the head's office.* There is a "book" in the head's office to which children are sent when they behave inappropriately in class. The book asks that they describe the events that led to their being sent from class. They discuss their entry with the head or with a member of their teaching team. We frequently ask children to write about an incident.

We wonder sometimes if we are successful in increasing a child's capacity for empathy. This remains an elusive goal. We think it is the most important, however. Robert Coles reminds us to "listen to the story-tellers." We talk about that often. Sometimes, we use the Town Meeting as a forum for children to begin unraveling their closely held stories.

Tom had never acknowledged to his friends here, even after 3 years, that his mother and father were deceased. One died in a gun fight, the other in prison of AIDS. One day in Town Meeting, we were discussing the AIDS quilt, which was coming to a nearby city. Tom asked if we could have a field trip. "There might be a part for my mother," he said.

Ben, every adult's dream of a teachable boy, had an IQ of more than 160. He got along fine with adults. With peers, he was a failure. His EQ—his "emotional intelligence"—was low. At a Town Meeting early in the year, Ben announced his goals for the coming months: "I have never been able to make friends," he said. "I do the wrong things. I hope I can change that." Ben continued to do the wrong things for the next 4 months, then he began to catch on. At the end-of-year meeting, he announced that he had achieved all of his goals for the year: He had learned to ski, he had climbed Mt. Marcy, and he had made friends. Back now for his second year, Ben has learned the social significance of occasional bad behavior. The work is never done.

LIFE SKILLS, COUNSELING, AND REPARENTING

A team of three people is charged with overseeing our SEL program: a social worker, a learning specialist, and a nurse. The somatic, cognitive, and emotional lives of children are, as we all now know, highly integrated. When we separate one from the others, for the sake of simplicity and manageable practice, we run into complications. This team teaches regular classes in "life skills" using case studies, ethical dilemmas, discussion of school and house issues, and published curricula that deal with conflict resolution, family and friendship issues, and self-image, as well as sex education, wellness, and metacognition. The SEL team carefully reads the records of each incoming student so that they may advise teachers of learning style variances, social skill deficits, family and cultural background, and health concerns. Some children are assigned to counseling or tutorial sessions as a regular part of their week.

COMMON MEALTIMES

Increasingly over the past 10 years, North Country has found in its population children to whom the common civilities of life, whether those of the dinner table or of interpersonal relations, have not been taught. At our school, we provide tables with adults who serve food and teach manners. Often we have to start at the beginning, for most children who arrive here have little experience with common mealtimes. Most children today don't sit at tables with a "head" and therefore don't acquire the behaviors that the ceremony of a shared meal inculcate. It was not carelessly that Shakespeare so often chose the ceremonial banquet as a way of revealing harmony or discord in a household or a kingdom. The communal meal has been the center point of civilization for as long as anyone can trace. The disappearance of a consistent and reliable symbol of order and authority in a child's life—for example, around the dinner table—may well be part of the difficulty today's children have with acknowledging adult authority.

Some of our most difficult and focused interactions with children occur around the table. Adult and child often lock in a conflict of wills; the working out of that conflict is instructional to the table as a whole and helpful to the child's maintaining his or her sense of safety and stability. Our children, like any others, test us to make sure that we are strong enough to protect them through the sometimes dangerous voyage of adolescence.

We hold hands in a sectarian moment of silence before each meal and at Town Meeting. Everyone is a part of this circle, we say, and children are safe in this circle. They wonder how safe? How far can they go and still be accepted? Will you still accept me if? Love me if? Sometimes the testing stretches us beyond our resiliency, and we send a child home. But rarely.

We engage children in conversation about their health, eating habits, hygiene, learning style, feelings, peer and family relationships, and sense of personal identity. The conversation is not the same, of course, with a 10-year-old as it is with a 14-year-old. But for each, it has the same ingredients and expresses the same desire to help build practical self-knowledge—the sort that allows her to recognize personal limits, recover from anger, imagine outcomes to alternative strategies, learn effective social behaviors, and live—if not always comfortably, then at least pragmatically—with the requirements of a social contract.

ANIMALS AND NATURE

Most of us can tell affecting and significant stories about children bonding with animals: Jack, during a painful bout of homesickness, took responsibility for 100 newborn chicks and took his sleeping bag to the brooder house so that he could be sure the chicks were safe. Seiji, the only Japanese boy in the school, so persuasively worried about our llama's loneliness that we acquired a second one. Paulette, who discovered that a mother goat was not nursing one of her newborn kids, stayed up all night with a bottle hoping to take that mother's place. Paulette had been adopted. Our animals are some of our best teachers. It is a long-established practice at the school that animals are fed first and people second. The reason we offer is that the animals are dependent on us for their care and shelter. The children occasionally modify this to say that the animals "trust us," and that trust must not be betrayed. Hidden in this attitude are values that we have not carefully enumerated but suspect may carry some residual value for parenting later in the child's life.

People learn through patterns, and there are few patterns that cannot be learned among the seasons. Here nature is our master teacher, revealing not only discrete truths, but also order, sequence, and balance that underlie the working of all things. Life assumes "her" natural proportions here; things are small enough and connected enough to make sense to a child. Finding sense in their world, children learn to make sense of themselves. The environment, "Mother Nature," plays many roles in this landscape. "She" is unpredictable (the ice storm of 1998 shut down our power, heat, and water), makes occasionally unreasonable demands (barn chores at 7 a.m. in the dark at 30 degrees below zero), challenges us (five peaks to be climbed in 14 hours), teaches trust (we have no outside lights; children navigate at night by starlight), entertains (snow forts, sledding, skating, swimming, lying in the grass), nourishes (a fresh-pulled carrot, maple syrup, fresh eggs gathered warm from nests), instructs (snowflake science, pond science, the Pumpkin Project), forces moral questions (the beaver dilemma), and inspires.

GREATER RESOURCES FOR SEL WHEN EMOTIONAL NEEDS INCREASE

With the work of CASEL as an example, we have recently undertaken an even more intentional program of social and emotional education. Each of us has taken on two or three children as advisees. The adviser's major task is to be helpful in the relationship of parent and child, to help each articulate goals for the year, and to audit the child's progress in meeting those goals. It is the task of the adviser to be informed on all aspects of the child's life at school and maintain a regular liaison with the child's parents or guardians. New teachers slowly learn to recognize in themselves the facile arrogance that comes so easily to a community of surrogate caretakers—the easy criticism and careless disdain that one can feel for a parent who may be seen to have "failed." We learn slowly about projection on the part of our children and imagine ourselves as rescuers. We bring, sometimes from our own lives, a passion for restitution, for making things right. Achieving objectivity about ourselves and our children is one of our most important and persistent tasks.

Objectivity is not easily gained in a community of adults who are quick to identify with a child and his or her feelings about a parent. We spend a lot of time relearning this. The obligation of an adviser is specifically one that involves listening to parents, hearing their concerns, and empathizing with their pain of separation, as well as that of the child. This probably is not a problem unique to boarding schools.

Children are like spiders, weaving the webs of their lives through a series of greater and lesser leaps into the unfamiliar. The beauty and durability of their architecture depends both on their virtuosity and on the firmness with which the web is anchored. We try to provide, in partnership with parents, good anchor points from which children may make their leaps and to which they can safely return. These anchors are our community, our environment, the evenness of our tempers, and the clarity and consistency of our beliefs.

We are successful on about the same average as thoughtful teachers in any school that values SEL work, that supports it with time and competent adults, and that maintains a community that is not itself at odds (structurally or philosophically) with the goals of civility.

CHAPTER TWELVE

Promoting Students' Social–Emotional and Intellectual Well-Being and the School as an Ecosystem

From Program to Way of Life

Chana Shadmi

Bilha Noy

The Psychological and Counseling Service ("Sherut Psychologi Yeutsi"—SHEFI) in the Israeli Ministry of

Education, Culture, and Sport is charged with promoting the wellness of all students and of the educational system as an ecosystem. This chapter reviews the process and activities of SHEFI, with a focus on the establishment of a section within SHEFI that combines units that previously implemented separate prevention and developmental programs. The new department incorporates a comprehensive developmental and preventive program based on a common goal: to promote the social–emotional and intellectual well-being of students and of the climate of our schools.

This process was accompanied by the difficulties and dilemmas typical of any change, particularly given the unique nature of the Psychological and Counseling Service as a body that combines two related professions, guidance counseling and school psychology. The lessons learned are instructive for those seeking to create large-scale, multidisciplinary, multisetting change that will lead to synergy between emotional intelligence (EQ) and IQ in schools.

PSYCHOLOGICAL COUNSELING SERVICE: FUNCTION, STRUCTURE, AND OBJECTIVES

SHEFI is charged with providing psychological and guidance counseling services for students, parents, and educators. The goal of the service is to assist the educational system in achieving its objectives. Alongside an emphasis on realizing learning potential and securing appropriate academic achievements, those involved with SHEFI believe that it is important to promote the emotional and social development of students, as a condition of their realizing their innate potential and as part of their positive adaptation and involvement in society at large. Through SHEFI, schools are also able to provide individual therapy and counseling services for students with special needs.

Most of the work of SHEFI is guided by a systemic approach that views the individual as part of a cluster of social systems—family, classroom, school, and community. As a body assisting policymakers at various levels in the Ministry of Education, SHEFI has several objectives:

1. To articulate processes for promoting growth (emotional, social, and cognitive) among the population of students as a whole, while recognizing differences and special needs of all students

2. To integrate psychological counseling into policy and activities to ensure the effectiveness of the educational approach

3. To make available to all principals methodologies, methods, and appropriately trained personnel to cope with the range of issues that SHEFI addresses, from four specific perspectives: that of individual students, that of the educational framework, that of the processes of teaching and learning, and that of the family and community

4. To make available to all principals indices and methods of evaluation that are applicable to the various issues that SHEFI addresses, enabling assessment of the educational system in these fields

5. To promote attention to "SHEFI considerations" in decisions and policies of various governmental ministries and authorities, ensuing that mental health implications are taken into account

SHEFI includes three sections that act to attain these goals: the School Psychological Service, which numbers 1,800 psychologists employed in 268 centers; the Guidance Counseling Section, comprising some 2,500 guidance counselors; and the Assistance and Prevention Programs Section, the establishment of which will be described next.

ESTABLISHING THE ASSISTANCE AND PREVENTION PROGRAMS SECTION: THE OPPORTUNITIES AND DIFFICULTIES OF INTRODUCING CHANGE

Until 3 years ago, eight programs operated within SHEFI: sex and family life education, drug and alcohol abuse prevention, violence prevention, child abuse prevention, improving learning processes, classroom climate, career development, and life skills. Separate administrative units and marketing mechanisms were established for each program, and each had its own team of counselors. Most of the programs were created as the result of political pressure following problems in the field; the order of the programs as listed here is the order in which they were introduced into the educational system.

The development of the life skills program in the early 1990s represented an attempt to establish a core program for all the other programs. This decision reflected a perception that the subject of life skills lay at the heart of any program and could provide a uniform base for all other programs. The life skills program was implemented mainly in elementary and junior high schools and grew from 75 schools in the first year to 850 schools operating the program this year. Reports from the field consistently reflect a high level of satisfaction with the programs. Teachers, who receive training from guidance counselors, operate the program. In an evaluation study of the program during its first 2 years, teachers reported that the program had enabled them to become better acquainted with their students and to talk with them about issues they had not addressed in the past. The program also enabled them to create numerous connection points to the curriculum, particularly regarding the humanities, the Bible, history, and literature. Despite the program's success in the field, it operated in isolation and was not connected to the other preventive programs.

A SINGLE FRAMEWORK IS NECESSARY

Establishment of the new section was a step toward unifying the programs under a single framework. Each of the programs operates as part of a comprehensive response aimed to ensure the well-being of the individual and the system. The following variables served as catalysts in the decision to introduce change.

Emotional Intelligence

Development of the concept of emotional intelligence and a greater appreciation of the importance of education involving the wider community have fueled changes in the perception of the function of guidance counseling and school psychology. These changes emphasize teamwork based on cooperation and focus less on the distinct character of each profession. This trend has also promoted cooperation between various programs in the field of mental health.

Multidisciplinary Approaches

The introduction of multidisciplinary approaches into education has influenced the reorganization of learning in the schools. The creation of core programs for content area subjects, and greater cooperation across subjects in issue-focused learning, led to the need to combine different prevention and life skills units into a comprehensive program integrated into the curriculum.

Competition for Instructional Time

Reductions of "teacher time" and "class time" available to each program created practical difficulties in implementing all the separate programs. Therefore, comprehensive intervention is needed, emphasizing, on the one hand, common aspects, while on the other focusing on the specific messages of each program.

Common Core of Problems

Results of surveys comparing risk behaviors among youth (e.g., drug and alcohol use, violence, premature sexual activity) have reflected the connection between these phenomena and the efficacy of interventions that address these issues as a whole (Harel, Kenny, & Rahav, 1998). These data enhanced the understanding of the need to create a comprehensive developmental program based on a synergistic approach to the various programs.

Promotion of Wellness As a Superordinate Goal

The adoption of holistic approaches in medicine, education, and organizations reflects a change in trends of intervention toward promoting wellness of individuals and of the organization within the population as a whole. Along with this, there is less emphasis on "immunization" and prevention against social hazards and diseases. This approach is nothing short of a revolution and has even been reflected in linguistic terms. Until recently, the literature has teemed with descriptions of the causes of illnesses and with proposed methodologies to be used for curing and repairing disturbances, but there had been relatively little attention paid to the well-being of individuals and organizations. This is now changing, with new emphasis on "wellness" and positive approaches that include, but go beyond, prevention (Cowen, 1994).

Influence Educational Policy

SHEFI recognized that to meets its goals, it would be necessary to influence educational policymakers at all levels with a view to encouraging them to pay attention to considerations of wellness.

Administrative Reorganization to Reflect Goals

A new SHEFI director introduced the following administrative changes designed to create synergy of goals, methods, and structure:

1. Creation of a process to consolidate the goals of SHEFI to guide policy and to ensure that work proceeded according to plans and that results were monitored

2. Introduction of a proactive approach to building strengths, reflected in new initiatives on policy, implementation, and monitoring in such fields as coping with learning disabilities and reducing the level of violence

3. Emphasis on teamwork among psychologists, counselors, and the staff in the Assistance and Prevention Programs Section to enhance the influence of SHEFI in the system and to provide an example of a collaborative process that we advocate

4. Making the creation of the Assistance and Prevention Programs Section a priority and designing it in such a way that it could consolidate various programs into proactive activities, while developing specialization to allow for prompt and effective reaction to specific situations as they arose

THE CONNECTION BETWEEN THE STRUCTURE OF THE SECTION AND ITS FUNCTION IN IMPLEMENTING SHEFI'S GOALS

The Assistance and Prevention Programs Section operates alongside and in cooperation with two other sections: the Counseling Section and the Psychology Section. Its functions are to provide SHEFI and the educational system with expertise and assistance in developing a comprehensive and holistic development program; to propose and assist in the development of preventive policy and to implement this policy in the system; and to provide professional training for a system preparing professional teams to operate the program in schools. To realize these goals, it was necessary to change the work foci in the following ways:

1. Where separate units within each section once operated their programs on a competitive basis, a sense of teamwork needed to be established to create a developmental program that provided a complete response involving all the units.

2. Where the exclusive concern of the sections previously was primary prevention, there needed to be additional specialization in secondary prevention (i.e., response to early signs of risk and crisis).

3. Where participants once worked mainly within one section, joint work with the other sections in areas of policy and program adjustment was needed to meet the unique needs of each district and school.

To achieve these goals, the Assistance and Prevention Section was created, in part with consultation from Dr. Maurice Elias of Collaborative for Academic, Social, and Emotional Learning. Structurally, the Assistance and Prevention Section and the units within it were not made subsidiary parts of the Counseling Section, but elevated to the status of an equivalent section combining members of various disciplines and offering its services both to the

Psychological and the Counseling sections. The structure of its units is as follows.

Developmental Unit (Holistic Team)

This unit was created by the unification of three groups: life skills counselors, classroom atmosphere counselors, and career counselors. The function of this unit is to lead a holistic process combining the developmental aspects of promoting well-being with the creation of supportive social environments and the promotion of empowering conditions. This unit is responsible for developing Life Skills and EQ, promoting a healthy school climate, building children's ability to cope with the various roles of life (family, career development, etc.), and providing an integrative foundation for focused aspects of prevention, such as drugs and alcohol. The unit also teaches counselors how to create foci of intervention based on an analysis of needs and developmental tasks, the composition of the population, diagnosis of the system and its educational approach, and how to make adaptations to existing curricula.

Preventive Units

The Preventive Units comprise the following areas of concern: violence prevention, drug and alcohol abuse and smoking prevention; prevention of child abuse; and sex and family life education. These units are responsible for developing methodologies and for providing the training for individuals to develop expertise in these fields. Each unit operates both separately and in the context of the other areas. They are responsible for integrating messages of prevention to promote overall quality of life and for operating focused prevention programs according to developmental needs and the needs of specific populations.

The Unit for the Improvement of Learning Skills

This unit is responsible for assisting the age-based divisions in the development of meaningful dialogue between learners and teachers relating to the learning process and the organization of learning and learning strategies. It also is responsible for attention to the pedagogical aspects of the developmental program.

Ad Hoc (Rapid Response) Unit

This new unit has been charged with providing a rapid response to new issues according to emerging needs in the educational system. For example, this unit has been particularly active in the context of violence and terror in Israeli schools and communities.

PREPARATION OF A CONSOLIDATED, DEVELOPMENTAL CURRICULUM

Creating a curriculum for the developmental program was one of the joint tasks undertaken by the heads of the Assistance and Prevention Section units, in cooperation with representatives from the Counseling Section and the Psychologists Section. The basis for preparation of the curriculum was taken from the approach of Emory Cowen (1994; see Figure 12.1). He identified five factors that promote mental health and a sense of "wellness," and these provided us with the organizational foundations around which we mapped program content. These five factors are a sense of competency and control over the course of life (intrapersonal), interpersonal relationships and attachments, acquiring age-appropriate abilities, being in wellness-enhancing environments, and having skills for effective coping in situations of stress, crisis, and difficulty. Clearly, while Cowen's concepts predated work in EQ, the two ideologies share great synergy.

The five factors defined the model of the "whole" we sought to produce, both through the comprehensive developmental curriculum and through focused preventive interventions. These factors were the means of creating a language common to all prevention program developers as well as to life skill curriculum developers. The factors in the model are interrelated, and therefore a program that emphasizes one factor can simultaneously relate to and promote the rest of the factors.

Figure 12.1   Five Pathways That Promote Mental Health and Wellness

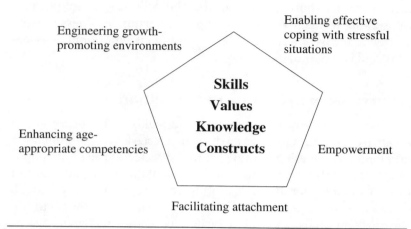

Source: These concepts have been adapted from Cowen (1994). The diagram appeared in "A Comprehensive Program for the Enhancement of Children's Psychological Wellness: A Meta-Cognitive Approach for Generating Psychoeducational Intervention Programs" by Tamar Erez, Osnat Binstock, Orly Seroussi, and Chana Shadmi (unpublished paper, 2001). Used with permission.

A Definition of Well-Being and Competence

A basis for defining well-being was provided by the definition drafted in 1970 by the Joint Commission on Mental Health of Children, which noted that mentally healthy persons are capable of seeing events and circumstances that affect themselves and their world and, in most cases, of coping with these realities. They are capable of accepting and controlling sexual and aggressive urges. They are capable of learning and then of implementing what they have learned; they have confidence in their own competence. They possess values according to which their lives are built. They have a sense of group affiliation, and they are confident of their identity. Socially and emotionally healthy individuals continue to develop throughout life and show flexibility in encountering new tasks and situations.

Thus wellness was defined not in negative terms, as the absence of mental illness, but rather according to the extent to which factors promoting well-being are present. An emphasis was placed on the synergistic presence of components as mutual factors, rather than as competitors. The definition is not phrased in absolute terms, but rather along a spectrum. Wellness may be viewed in terms of a range of biopsychosocial, emotional, intellectual, and behavioral manifestations.

A Curriculum to Capture the Definition

To translate this understanding into reality, it was necessary to create a curriculum to serve as the centerpiece for a comprehensive and long-term developmental program directed at the entire population, rather than only toward at-risk populations. The curriculum provides "tools" for those operating the program in the school: counselors, principals, and teachers. By means of the curriculum, the program can be adapted to the developmental and environmental needs of the various student populations. The structure of the curriculum includes not only content, but also congruent processes by which content is selected and conveyed. It must meet academic criteria and be "user-friendly." Finally, it must be open to observation and measurement; components and processes must be defined in such a manner as to enable the development of evaluation indices.

The curriculum structure can be understood by an overview of its chapters, as follows:

• *Rationale behind the preparation of the developmental program.* This chapter includes the program's basic assumptions, goals, and principles of operation; a description of the characteristics of the school that functions according to the program; presentation of the learning process; a selection of tools for use in implementing the program; and a list of capabilities and know-how required on the part of those acting as consultants or who are trainers and implementers of the program.

• *Development of capabilities according to age.* This chapter describes the perception of different ages as periods that are sensitive to specific intervention on particular subjects, the characteristic dilemmas of each age, key developmental situations, and the place of significant adults (parents, teachers) in the developmental process.

• *Diagnosis and evaluation.* This chapter includes guiding questions on diagnosing the school system and the school's educational approach. It also provides information on academic content that will assist in emotional and social learning and enhancing the relationship between IQ and EQ. Finally, additional guiding questions help to diagnose the school population and to adapt the program to different populations.

- *Guidelines for using the curriculum.* This chapter describes the development of a program through different organizing elements, including student competencies, values, life situations, dilemmas, and current events. Also discussed is the use of life skills texts written for elementary schools and the use of the middle school program.

- *Defining the space that enables growth.* This chapter describes how to create an environment that enables basic needs to be met, including security, belonging, capability, and autonomy. Also discussed are the environmental characteristics of the safe school, the importance of mutual respect and basic values for the existence of interpersonal relations, the school as a learning community, and involvement in the school of the broader community through operation of the curriculum program.

- *Mapping content according to fields.* This chapter describes the importance of a sense of capability and control of the course of life (interpersonal), of connections and relationships between individuals and social relations (interpersonal), and of coping effectively with difficulties, pressure, and crises. Each of these fields is detailed according to the following questions: Why develop this component? What need does it meet? For what does it provide an infrastructure? What will happen as the result of intervention in this component? Which skills, attitudes, and types of knowledge should be developed? How can this component be connected to the subjects studied in the school curriculum? What additional concepts should be addressed in this context? Also included is consideration of dilemmas facing teachers and parents guiding the teaching of each component.

- *Mapping content according to key intervention foci for each age.* This chapter describes the five age groups chosen for intervention: K–Grade 2; Grades 3–4; Grades 5–6; Grades 7–9; and Grades 10–12. For each age group, a number of characteristic foci were chosen around which we propose that learning be organized. For example, foci for early childhood include starting kindergarten and moving on to Grade 1, playgroups, children and their families, the class as a social group, controlled consumption of the media, and dyadic and group relationships. A similar set of issues serves as the focus for each age group, framed in a developmentally appropriate manner. Each of these foci is detailed according to the following guiding questions: Which skills and what knowledge would we like to develop that will foster a sense of competency, attachments and interpersonal relations, and positive coping with stress, crisis, and difficult situations? What kind of environment should we create to enable learning? What will happen as a result of intervention in this area? To which other areas do we want to relate? Which concepts need to be clarified? These questions serve as key points in the creation of interventions.

Other sections cover the integration of special subjects and targeted prevention areas into the developmental program, give suggestions for when and how to provide these targeted interventions across the grade levels, and provide cross listings and content maps for health promotion interventions and focused intervention in emergencies—all concepts that are part of the program. Annotated references are also included.

Description of the Curriculum As Delivered to Students

Life Skills Texts for Elementary School

Life skills texts are published in three volumes, Grades 1–2, Grades 3–4, and Grades 5–6. Each volume includes four sections: an introduction and three chapters of specific lesson activities. Within the introduction, the first chapter, "Capabilities," includes self-development, social skills, interpersonal communication, assertiveness, problem solving and decision making, and coping with stress and change. The second chapter, "Developmental Issues," includes learning processes, sex education and family life education, and professional development and careers. The third chapter, "Preventive Issues," includes preventing drug and alcohol abuse and smoking, preventing violence in school, and coping with situations of child abuse. The texts also include the theoretical rationale, suggestions for integrating the various units in the program, suggestions for integrating the life skills program and the academic curriculum, adaptations and comments from

Jewish sources, and suggestions for integrating Israeli Educational Television broadcasts.

Life Skills Program for Middle School sections: "Windows to Adolescence"

The life skills program for middle school sections constitutes a continuation of the elementary program but is ordered differently. The central theme behind the organization of the written program is the "image of the desirable adult," as published in a collection of position papers by the Pedagogic Secretariat and in the Memorandum of the Director-General of the Ministry of Education.

The program is structured according to the analogy of the Windows computer operating system. Based on an analysis of the adult character and extensive focus-group discussions with youth, educators, parents, and professionals, 15 main "windows" were selected:

- Family
- Learning
- School as an organization
- Career
- Peer group
- Society
- Individual identity
- Worldview and values
- Capabilities
- Transitions
- Situations of stress
- Danger and crisis
- Life in the environment of psychoactive substances
- Health
- Leisure

Each window includes the following: rationale sentences connecting the issue to the character of the adult; a pool of key questions for discussions relating to the subject of that window; suggestions for sources that implementers and students can consult, including theoretical material and referrals to activities; and referrals to other, related windows that are recommended to be opened simultaneously. Each main window opens onto secondary windows relating to the characteristics of the age group; the functions of adolescents within the different circles in which they act; the development of individual identity, worldview, and values; the development of life skills; and coping with common life situations encountered during adolescence.

The windows approach enables the derivation of specific programs for prevention and life skills development, sex and family life education, improving learning processes, career development, and improving class atmosphere, but it does so in an integrative, flexible way that is linked to ongoing areas of particular relevance to students. In addition, special attention is given to applications related to Jewish education and to life in the Arab sector. The program, which represents a collaboration of all parts of SHEFI under the leadership of the Holistic Unit, is published both in book form and on the SHEFI Web site (www.education.gov.il/shefi/ [in Hebrew]).

CONSOLIDATION OF THE WORK OF SHEFI IN THE AREAS OF VIOLENCE PREVENTION AND CONNECTIONS WITH DISTRICT SCHOOLS AROUND EMOTIONAL INTELLIGENCE

Violence Prevention

The Ministry of Education, Culture, and Sport decided to address "The Right to Dignity and the Duty to Respect" as its central theme to introduce the new millennium. This was chosen in response to a rising rate of violence in the culture and a concern to keep it from the schools, as well as to prepare students to be nonviolent in their communities. As a professional body, all sections of SHEFI are taking part in a holistic effort to provide principals (at all levels) with methodologies, methods, professional staff, indices, and evaluation tools relating to the subject of violence in the education system. Recent and ongoing activities include the following:

- Inviting academics who study violence to participate in a joint discussion on the topic
- Preparing documents presenting policy recommendations for the Ministry of Education at the national, district and local, and individual school levels
- Writing director-general's memoranda intended to empower schools to take responsibility for addressing this subject
- Connecting with key figures in local school districts to recruit the broader community to joint activities to address violence
- Publishing a bulletin (*Shefiton;* published September 1998) for counselors and psychologists devoted to the subject of violence in the education system. (The bulletin includes reviews of research undertaken in Israel and around the world on this subject, a review of various tools used in diagnosing and mapping the phenomenon, articles describing various strategies for preventing and treating violence, and examples of initiatives in the field by schools and psychological services that have created change in the level of violence. The publication also was distributed to principals.)
- Training teams of counselors to act as mentors for professionals in creating school atmospheres that encourage growth and reduce violence in the context of other preventive efforts
- Building an index for examining the level of violence in schools and issuing a kit for school principals providing guidance in self-diagnosis of the level of violence in the school and identification of foci of violence
- Preparing a position paper by members of the section articulating how human dignity is addressed within the framework of the life skills developmental program and as part of the special subjects in which they specialize, toward placing the issue of violence prevention in a broader, integrative, wellness perspective
- Enhancing SHEFI participation in public committees and other governmental efforts to address violence

SHEFI-District Connections: Binat Halev/EQ–Life Skills 2000 Comes to Tel Aviv

The special development and implementation of the life skills program in schools are influenced by emerging trends in the various districts. No effort is made to impose a single model. We encourage the special development of the program and the creation of connections to central issues being led by the district. An example of broad-based cooperation between SHEFI and the district may be found in the development and implementation of emotional intelligence in the Tel Aviv district.

At the initiative of the district superintendent of schools at the time, Dr. Josef Levi, it was decided that the development of emotional intelligence would be integrated both directly and indirectly into the curricula of district schools. To this end, several localities were chosen for the introduction of an experimental program: Kiryat Ono, Ramat Hasharon, Tel Aviv, Givatayim, and Herzliya. The base or foundation of the program is the life skills curriculum, which teaches the basic skills of emotional intelligence. But each school and community creates its own "house of learning" on this foundation through the ways in which it creates a context for the skills to become part of the entire educational program and the life of each child, classroom, school building, and neighborhood.

"Binat Halev"—the Wisdom of the Heart—describes the way in which each school develops an approach to school reform and transformation that touches each faculty member and each student. Each locality develops its own unique model, assisted by professionals from SHEFI. A district steering committee is established, including district and SHEFI personnel. At the same time, local steering committees, including representatives from education and other aspects of the municipal government, are established to lead the process of change and to bring it to the level of the community, as well as the school. The underlying goal is to introduce the language of emotional intelligence in all the district's activities and among all partners: local authorities, inspectors, principals, school and kindergarten teachers, students and parents. Through this activity, a district declares its responsibility to develop the emotional and social aspects of students, alongside intellectual aspects.

DIFFICULTIES AND CHALLENGES

The process of change undergone by SHEFI in general, and by the sections in particular, has entailed numerous difficulties and challenges. Recognition of the difficulties, and a willingness to develop meaningful dialogue about these difficulties, is what transforms them into challenges. These challenges have broad relevance for those administering changes in programs at the national, state, district, and local levels.

"Space" Versus "Territory"

The transition from separate to joint work among the sections and the units sometimes creates a feeling that someone's "territory" is being "invaded." Forging joint work demands that the different sections and units define the distinct added value of each and the areas of overlap that offer a chance for teamwork and cooperation. Strong, persistent, and visionary leadership is essential for this to take place.

Development and Training Versus Implementation

Discrepancies sometimes emerge between the development of programs and inservice training and the actual implementation of programs in schools. The quantifiable variable is the extent to which the investment in the development of professionals actually reaches the field in general and each child in particular. A key issue in this context is determining the target population and goal. Is training intended to empower professionals in the field (counselors and psychologists), is it intended to have a direct and clear impact on schools, or should it accomplish both? Genuine change requires a dedication to ensuring that school and child-based impact takes place.

Extent of Coordination Across Different Levels

The following are examples of issues that are part of continuing discussions: (a) Is the level of implementation of a program happening according to the original intentions of the planners?

(b) Is the implementation of a program characterized by flexibility? Do various collaborators tend to listen to each other and to change accordingly? (c) Which work procedures between the teams focused on curriculum and program development and those focused on implementation are most effective? (d) When does the Assistance and Prevention Unit, as a development body, get drawn into the effort to meet short-term needs, and how does it balance long-term and short-term concerns? (e) What is the responsibility of SHEFI as a centralized organization to initiate processes in the field? What will be the impact of trends toward the school-based management approach on attempts to have a coherent national response to issues of prevention and life skills development?

Connection Between Specific Specialization and the Comprehensive Program

Should separate programs be operated for each prevention, life skills, and special interest area, or should a broad-based holistic program be created, including key prevention messages, with direct prevention messages conveyed through focused interventions within the overall program? The transition from a separate "unit" structure to a holistic approach creates tension and controversy, as well as opportunity.

CONCLUSION

Opting for a process of change was not the result of a unanimous decision. Doubt, hesitation, and compromise accompanied it. This was and is clearly a journey rather than a one-time event; the rules of the game as we knew them are being broken, and we devise new ones as we go along. The understanding that uncertainty and difficulty are part of the process and the willingness to face them actively make this a joint venture of creativity. As we share the experience of creating new products, the process of change and collaboration is clarified further. Yet we know all too well that circumstances can and will arise that provide continuous and daunting challenges. Nonetheless, through our ongoing evaluation efforts and attempts at anticipating future needs, we feel that children benefit from the changes we are making, and this is our ultimate goal.

REFERENCES

Cowen, E. L. (1994). The enhancement of psychological wellness: Challenges and opportunities. *American Journal of Community Psychology, 22,* 144–179.

Harel, J., Kenny, D., & Rahav, G. (1998). *Youth in Israel: Social welfare, health and risk behaviors from an international perspective.* Jerusalem: Brookdale Institute. (In Hebrew)

PART THREE

Making It Happen in Your School

Implementation Guidelines

INTRODUCTION

Learning From Others, Connecting to Others

Maurice J. Elias

Harriett Arnold

Cynthia Steiger Hussey

IMPLEMENTING SCHOOLWIDE INITIATIVES

Having a vision of success in bringing social–emotional learning and emotional intelligence (SEL/EQ) into one's school or system is a necessary but insufficient condition for achieving that success. Much depends on the process of turning one's ideas into action.

The Collaborative for Academic, Social, Emotional, Learning (www.CASEL.org) has devoted extensive time to studying the implementation of school-based efforts to promote social–emotional skills; to create caring, safe, drug-free communities of learners; and to prevent an array of problem behaviors.

CASEL's approach has been field-based, derived from many years of observing and working in schools as they have sought to carry out SEL/EQ curricula and schoolwide procedures. Many of their findings were summarized in *Promoting Social and Emotional Learning: Guidelines for Educators* (Elias et al., 1997). These guidelines, which are in a constant state of analysis and refinement, are summarized in the section that follows. This version is based on the most current work, at the time of this writing, by Hank Resnik and the CASEL Leadership Team.

GUIDELINES FOR EFFECTIVE SEL PROGRAMS

1. *Effective EQ schools are built around specific, developmentally sequenced instruction in life skills and social–emotional competencies using evidence-based approaches.* EQ is a skill area, not a disposition or set of character attributes. As a skill area, it requires specific instruction every year, much as math and reading do. It cannot be infused into other areas or it will lack the salience needed for children to access and use their EQ skills in a wide variety of situations, especially stressful ones, when no adult is present to prompt them. And like other subject areas, it is least likely to be internalized if it is presented in isolation or if it is not coordinated with instruction in related areas. Examples of those areas include health education; efforts to prevent, smoking, alcohol, drug, and steroid use; HIV/AIDS prevention; violence prevention; and citizenship and service education. Furthermore, EQ strategies need to be incorporated into disciplinary procedures and efforts to remediate identified problems in students.

2. *Communications between school leaders and staff members and among the school, parents and families, and the community must emphasize the relationship of SEL/EQ to academic success.* It is important that school leaders not allow themselves to be passive in light of the tyranny of negative publicity around schools and test scores. Sheldon Berman, superintendent in Hudson, Massachusetts, found that parents and community members were at least as interested in having children living in the community who were kind, caring, and nonviolent as they were in having kids who were smart. Berman's point was that schools and communities need

not choose; it is possible to have both. He saw that communications about his SEL/EQ programs and activities were not only sent home on a regular basis but also provided to local newspapers. The coverage allowed parents and other community members to understand what the schools were doing that had clear relevance to the enhancement of community life.

3. *Effective EQ schools provide their EQ-building efforts with clear administrative support, adequate staffing, attention to infrastructure, sufficient time for implementation, and stable funding.* It is important that the district administration, school board, and educators' unions show explicit support for the design and implementation of EQ in schools. Curriculum leaders need to ensure that EQ curricula and related activities are aligned with district goals and relevant state and national standards. (The CASEL Web site will serve as an ongoing resource to assist in these efforts.) SEL/EQ cannot be an add-on. It must be someone's clear responsibility, and that someone will need access to a budget, resources for training and supervision, and administrative support. (There is an additional element to this that will be discussed in a concluding section.)

4. *Classroom-based SEL/EQ instruction serves as a launching pad for the use of SEL/EQ skills throughout the school day and in school-linked activities.* A launching pad provides a powerful send-off, and so it is not uncommon to find that schools with effective SEL/EQ programs engage students as active partners in creating a classroom atmosphere characterized by caring, responsibility, trust, and a commitment to learning and service. More than that, there is a clear expectation created that what is being learned are skills for sound character, which means that children are expected to use their EQ on the playground, at dismissal, on the bus, and on class trips. This expectation is part of what it takes to shift norms in schools to ones in which learning, caring, leading, and striving for a productive future are not nerdy, but typical. Two middle schools in Ridgewood, New Jersey, adopted innovative SEL/EQ norms. At George Washington Middle School, the community knows that the school is "a Learning Place, where Caring is shown, Dreams are born, and Leaders are made," and academics and school activities are organized around those themes. At Benjamin Franklin Middle School, students learn that, "You are the news," a powerful metaphor enacted in an extensive media-based

approach to SEL but even more widely affirming that the school is about them and that their deeds define who they are and what their school is and will be.

5. *In EQ schools, skills from formal SEL instruction in the class-room are continually transferred to everyday life and reinforced in all aspects of the school day and throughout the school community.* For SEL/EQ to have a powerful impact, it is important for efforts to extend outside the classroom and into academic subject areas; with a focus on creating positive climate, grade level themes are carried through into special projects and other schoolwide activi-ties that give visibility to SEL/EQ efforts. In addition, the approaches and skills used in SEL/EQ curricula should be coordi-nated with mental health, health, and other support services in the school district and community for children and youth. Finally, cultural sensitivity to sociodemographically diverse students and communities is essential when planning SEL/EQ activities in the school and community. Synergy allows a strong, consistent message to be conveyed.

6. *Active involvement of parents and family members in many different aspects of the students' learning is a way to bring EQ into the home.* Schools need to review their patterns of regular communi-cation with parents and families and strive to make them more effective and inclusive. Programs and support resources that will help build families' EQ skills and sensitivities only serve to help children come to school ready to learn and to contribute. Yet these efforts must also respect cultural differences and build on family strengths and values.

7. *An infrastructure to allow coordinated, sustained SEL/EQ efforts in schools includes well-planned, high-quality professional development and supervision at all levels of administration and instruction.* Someone needs to have clear responsibility for EQ enhancement in school buildings and in a district overall. Superintendents and principals can be so charged, but often their duties and backgrounds do not make them the best choice. Therefore, a designated committee or individual who will coordinate social–emotional development considerations is associated with long-term success of SEL/EQ in schools. Duties include focusing on continued training needs for new and experienced staff members, arranging for coaching and other teacher supports, and emphasizing and operationalizing peer

leadership, teamwork, and mutual support among school staff in all aspects of SEL programming.

8.   *There is an ethical and practical responsibility to ensure that formal and informal SEL/EQ activities have clear implementation and outcome criteria and are monitored regularly to ensure that they are carried out as planned and that their desired outcomes are achieved.*

The key question for administrators to be asking of themselves and their staff is, "How will we know when our efforts are successful?" Indicators of progress or problems must be used or developed that make sense to the staff. But time must be allowed for reasonable progress. It is also important to heed the words of veteran principal Tom Schuyler, who said, "That which is valued is checked up on." Therefore, procedures need to be put in place to ensure that SEL/EQ responsibilities are being carried out as planned. This can include methods such as checking lesson plans and periodically collecting activity feedback sheets, as well as having time for reports on SEL/EQ as part of grade level, subject area, and overall faculty meetings. Feedback from consumers is also important (i.e., staff members who implement, children who are recipients, and families and community groups that are involved). Summer curriculum development time is an excellent way to pull together feedback and make modifications for improvement. Results should regularly be shared with the school community and parents.

A STRATEGY FOR IMPLEMENTING THE GUIDELINES

The chapters in Part III of this book provide clear examples of different ways to accomplish the task of making SEL/EQ a reality in one's school. For educational administrators, these guidelines can be a source of information about what has worked in practice. They can serve as guard rails and organizers for one's efforts. But one essential point that CASEL has come to understand is the following: Successful, enduring, high-quality implementation of EQ + IQ in schools requires mentoring and personal contact with those who have made it happen in their schools or districts, preferably schools and districts similar to one's own.

Although the chapters have been written to illuminate the path taken, as well as what the destinations look like, many educational administrators will want more specific implementation guidance. In addition to the expertise and experience available from the authors and editors of this book, administrators seeking mentoring and peer support can also look to CASEL. To facilitate sharing of experiences as one's work in SEL/EQ proceeds, CASEL has created a network of superintendents and other educational administrators.

In addition, CASEL has set up a listserv on its Web site for a range of educators who are implementing SEL/EQ in their classrooms or schools. In these ways, CASEL attempts to facilitate direct contact between aspiring and experienced implementers. The latter have invariably encountered and overcome the same sets of obstacles that often stop fledgling SEL/EQ efforts in their tracks. Representative obstacles documented by CASEL (Elias et al., 1997) include the following:

- "There is not enough time in the curriculum."
- "We are accountable to standardized tests, not social–emotional needs."
- "This is the work of guidance counselors, social workers, and school psychologists."
- "It's the parents' job, and they should be doing it, not us."
- "This has not been part of my training, and I am not qualified to carry it out."

Finding a human contact and source of support for initiating and sustaining SEL/EQ efforts play a large role in overcoming these obstacles, as well as others linked to initiating and sustaining any school change effort.

Knowing the kinds of information that will be discussed in the chapters in Part III is also highly useful. For example, the implementation cycle requires about 2 to 3 years to get a curriculum program established in several grades or to initiate a buildingwide SEL/EQ plan. Moving into adjacent grade levels and coordinating across buildings takes an additional year or two, and moving to a district level realistically is a 5- to 7-year process. Once in place, however, IQ + EQ becomes the basic operating modality of one's educational system—a rich reward of transformation as a return on systematic, sustained, supported efforts.

Having an ongoing forum for support and tangible assistance and problem solving can often make the difference between implementation success and failure. What has distinguished the contributors in this book is their unwavering commitment to their vision of implementing high-quality SEL/EQ in their schools as an essential complement to their academic efforts. They are also singled out by their willingness to network, borrow, adapt, and refine and improve their efforts continually as changing student needs and staff resources dictate. Resource B contains additional resources to help administrators find support for beginning, improving, or expanding, SEL/EQ efforts. We wish you support and success.

REFERENCE

Elias, M. J., Zins, J. E., Weissberg, R. P., Frey, K. S., Greenberg, M. T., Haynes, N. M., Kessler, R., Schwab-Stone, M. E., & Shriver, T. P. (1997). *Promoting social and emotional learning: Guidelines for educators*. Alexandria, VA: Association for Supervision and Curriculum Development.

C H A P T E R   T H I R T E E N

A Vision of Schools With Heart and Spirit

How to Get There

Linda Lantieri

RUSSIAN JACK ELEMENTARY SCHOOL, ANCHORAGE, ALASKA

It is springtime in Anchorage. Russian Jack is an elementary school that has been part of a particular social and emotional learning (SEL) program—the Resolving Conflict Creatively Program (RCCP)—for more than a decade. The sun is bright and warm; the flowers are blooming in contrast to the not-so-distant mountain peaks that peer over the city with a winter-wonderland splendor.

Upon entering Russian Jack, one can't help but notice a sign posted on the entrance doorway. It reads, "Our mission at Russian Jack, a school of cultural diversity, is to ensure that each student is actively involved in their learning, while developing a positive sense of self and becoming a productive citizen who will contribute to society in a meaningful way."

Continuing down the hallway, to the right there is a large glass display case. Inside are myriad art projects, bright colorful masks, and drums. A sign above it reads, "These masks and drums are representative of the culture of the Inuit people of Alaska. They were made by our Young Ambassadors, students dedicated to promoting a deeper understanding of the rich cultural diversity of the children at Russian Jack Elementary School."

Up the stairs toward the second floor, a huge banner is in view, with the letters P-E-A-C-E—large, multicolored letters sewn over a pastel backdrop. It is magnificent. Young people probably read this several times a day as they go back and forth to the library and their classrooms; adults read it, too.

Teachers and children alike are working in groups, talking and sharing ideas. Classroom walls display several indicators that social and emotional learning is front and center at this school. "Put-up" charts line walls. "I-Messages" and "Active Listening" are listed as tools to be used for communication in the classroom. There is a calmness in the air, not the frenzy one can sometimes feel in schools.

Recess begins on the playground. It is a warm and clear day. The sun is up and shining almost all day at this time of the year: The children are playful and carefree. Mediators stand by in the lunchroom and outdoors. Several times a conflict begins to erupt, but mediators intervene immediately. The library mediation room is available in case it gets too cold to mediate outside.

These images from Anchorage offer hints of what can happen when an educational vision that recognizes the full range of human qualities possessed by our students is put into practice. This chapter touches on some of the things administrators and teams of teachers can do to transform a school's culture, drawing from my own experience as an elementary school assistant principal and director of a middle school, both in New York City, as well as from my experience as the founding director of the Resolving Conflict Creatively Program (RCCP), a comprehensive SEL program.

ENVISIONING SCHOOLS WITH HEART AND SPIRIT

Amidst the social crises of the 1980s and 1990s, we waited for young people to really get in trouble, even kill each other, before we responded with programs to create safe schools. More recently, we have seen a number of high-profile killings—including multiple murders linked to suicide by the perpetrators—among young people in the more affluent suburbs. These environments differ, as do the particulars of each individual case of "senseless" violence, but the common threads include fatalism, despair, and a lack of human connectedness. If the lessons learned from the violence of the late 1990s was insufficient, certainly the events of September 11, 2001, and their aftermath should teach us not to wait for more and more young people to lose their sense of community and purpose before we invite heart and spirit into education.

What would it mean to nurture experiences in intentional ways so that our classrooms could be places that facilitate emotional, social, and spiritual growth? In the schools of heart and spirit that I envision, the following would be true:

- The uniqueness and inherent value of every individual would be honored, and education would be seen as a lifelong process.
- Students and teachers alike would be engaged in inquiry, exploring and learning about what has heart and meaning for themselves. Different ways of knowing would be respected—those for which we could test and others too subjective to be measured—and we would pay as much attention to whether a student has a sense of his or her purpose in life as we do to his or her SAT scores.
- Schools leaders would shift from a centralized concept of power to approaches that help individuals and groups to self-organize.
- We add to the kind of "school spirit" that comes from winning a football game a greater concern with the spirit of collaboration and partnership and an appreciation of diversity within the school community.
- There would be a place and time for silence and stillness to help us face the chaos and complexity of life yet stay in touch with inner truth and the web of interconnectedness.
- We would provide all students and educators with outlets to put to use their gifts of intuition, imagination, and creativity.

- We would see the organization and mission of the school as reflective of the pursuit of social justice.

In short, I believe we need to see schools as active and alive organisms that place a high value on self-knowledge, healthy interpersonal relationships, the building of community, and care for our planet. These goals are not incompatible with the pursuit of academic excellence—indeed, they foster it. Without care, respect, and kindness, what purpose does intellectual competence serve?

As school leaders across the country realize the need for this work, I first encourage them to look within and ask themselves where they would like their schools to be. Schools embracing an SEL program know it isn't a quick fix, but a long-term commitment to building a new school culture. Arlene, a principal in New Jersey, explains why these efforts are worth it.

> This work has made a difference in my district, my school, and in my personal life. No other effort has touched so many people in my professional world and become so much a part of them—I can say with confidence that what has been learned will outlast our contact with the trainers. The language of RCCP has become woven into how we talk about what we do and how we care for one another in ways that no other approach I know has ever done.

When school leaders begin making a commitment to SEL, they start to realize that any real, long-lasting change isn't going to happen unless it becomes a part of the school culture—the ideologies, philosophies, expectations, attitudes, and practices important to the members of the school. What is the climate of this school like? How do the people act toward one another? Is there a lot of aggression? Is there an atmosphere of trust? Do people celebrate their differences and work toward collaborative problem solving? School culture affects every decision that is made. Ideally, it is the thread that holds schools together—a very durable thread, like the kind that is used to sew on buttons and adjust hems—the kind that doesn't easily break.

CHANGING SCHOOL CULTURES: SEEING THE RESULTS OF SEL

So how does SEL affect a school's culture? The following shows what a successful SEL program looks like.

Relationships Become Transformed

Young people and adults talk with a new level of articulation and passion about issues of diversity and about how to resolve conflict, manage emotions, and express feelings. And a transformation in the relationships people establish with others emerges from the self-reflection fostered by this work.

Problem Solving Is Commonplace

A problem-solving approach to daily school conflict is commonplace. It would be expected at a staff meeting for people to show respect for each other by managing their emotions, calmly stating their own views, and listening carefully and actually considering the viewpoints of others. In schools where this work has taken root, there are many opportunities to increase open communication among all sectors of the school community. There is an unspoken code that "at this school we talk about issues, we don't shove them under the table."

Diversity Is Respected and Valued

True respect and valuing of diversity permeate schools with a commitment to SEL. Young people and adults realize that the ways in which we interpret conflict and communication styles is very much influenced by cultural background, gender, and personal style, and they think twice before they jump to conclusions or use racial slurs to discriminate. They have the skills to "separate the people from the problem" and use these skills in their interactions. So there's a widely observed decrease in negative stereotypes as everyone becomes more accepting of differences, which opens communication between students, teachers, administrators, and parents as well.

Norms Do Not Support Violence or Bias

In schools that implement SEL, there is a vigilance about changing social norms that support violent behavior. Everything that happens in the school—the curriculum, the daily bulletins, the school activities, the discipline procedures—all state clearly that violence is not okay. Teachers talk with young people about the issues they are confronting. They explore together the alternatives and consequences to their actions. Together, they build a "culture of safety," a feeling of emotional and physical security. As the environment grows more cooperative and caring, the use of skills learned by adults and young people increases.

There are strong sanctions against violence and bias-related incidents. Weapons are grounds for expulsion. Derogatory racial comments are viewed as precursors to possible violent actions. They are not slid under the carpet, but are addressed when they arise, through open communication or constructive disciplinary action. Fighting is handled decisively and constructively, and not with a knee-jerk reaction of suspension.

Administrators struggle with the issue of school suspension. They know that suspending a student does nothing to change his or her behavior. At times, it does create a safer learning environment for others, particularly when a young person's actions consistently interrupt the teaching–learning process. But young people who are suspended are sent out into the community with few resources to change their ways and work themselves back into the school environment. So teachers strive to reduce the conflicts that result in suspendable actions. Because they are preventive in their approach, fewer issues blow up in the classroom. In-school suspension rooms can also be very effective, when they are used as places for teacher and student to be apart, cool off, and problem solve. Teachers, too, need to be willing to regroup and find ways that will help to reduce or extinguish the negative behavior.

When a student absolutely has to be suspended or expelled for a serious offense, it is important to provide opportunities for that student to receive the help he or she needs. Today we are seeing an increase in alternative schools as placements for students who have been removed from the regular education system, yet these students need to be given the opportunity to learn skills in how to manage their emotions and resolve conflicts nonviolently and creatively—and to learn that these skills are seen as core components of their educational experience. The focus needs to be on moving from punishment to positive discipline, in whatever way that can happen. A suspended student's time may be better spent learning social competency skills, doing community service, or receiving home teaching.

Democracy and Teamwork Flourish

Another notable feature of such schools is that power is shared in a spirit of creating a democratic environment. Principals and other administrators involved in SEL develop their skills in communication and group dynamics. They attend introductory training sessions, management retreats, and advanced workshops, and so do their staff members. They all know that organizations are healthier and consequently more successful when leadership is facilitative—when power is shared among the people in the organization.

Teamwork becomes the modus operandi for getting things done, and becoming an administrator at a peaceable school requires a whole reevaluation of how decisions are made. If we encourage openness and truth and the sharing of information, we have to be willing to make decisions based on clear observational criteria. It's then more difficult to be discriminatory, because it's usually subjective criteria that shut certain people out of opportunities. We can claim to have certain values and principles, but until our actions actually operationalize these ways of being, we fall short. And this shift doesn't come easily.

Although many factors influence the shaping of a school's culture in this way, such schoolwide change depends on three factors in particular: trusting relationships, commitment on the part of members of the school community, and a way for this community to take ownership of the process.

BUILDING RELATIONSHIPS, ESTABLISHING COMMITMENT, AND CREATING OWNERSHIP

School leaders who have undertaken the task of shifting a school's culture already realize the importance of working to build relationships. They ask themselves, How do people relate to each other in the school community and in what ways must this change? Relationships between individual adults, between individual students, and between adults and students become mutually supportive and strengthened through a commitment to the peaceable school. Through understanding, empathy, and respect for each other, a cooperative school spirit is established.

Just before Roberta became principal of P.S. 75 in Manhattan some years ago, her staff had lost trust—trust in the leadership, trust in each other. The school had no backbone, nothing to tie it together. She decided to get involved with RCCP as a way to bring this school together. "People didn't have trust in this place. They didn't trust children. They didn't trust parents. They didn't trust each other," she says. "There was no such thing as a staff party. I felt that this place needed a lot of support. But I also felt they needed a method in which to communicate and do things."

Young people recognize the importance of the quality of school relationships, too. Matt, a student mediator from Vista, California, said one day, "I think what's best about this school is the respect we kids get from the adults here. They care about how we think and what we have to say." Responses to a survey administered to students at Myrtle Banks Elementary School in New Orleans pointed across the board to the importance of the bonds students felt with their teachers (Patti, 1996). When asked what students liked best about their school, nearly every fifth- and sixth-grade student said something positive about their teachers and that they felt teachers cared about them. Interestingly enough, the dedication of teachers at this same school was reflected in their own statements: "I've been here for 15 years, and although these children come here with so many problems, I could never go teach anywhere else. These children need us here. For some of them, we're the only family they have." Clearly, relationship building is a priority in this school.

Having a common purpose and commitment is also crucial to long-term effectiveness, a fact borne out by the literature on school change. To develop these commonalities, school staff have to create an environment in which they can discover what they really care about, and then they have to get together so they can talk about their visions. When schools decide to begin this work, they first talk a lot—and listen, too. Involving all the key stakeholders—teachers, students, parents, and administrators—in this process early on ensures that the plan and direction of building a comprehensive SEL effort is understood and embraced by all.

But getting to core values, the deeply held beliefs that individuals collectively agree to put at the foundation of all they do in a school, is a long-term process. This vision of what a school believes and wants to be for its young people grows over time. Trying to decide in a few meetings what a school is all about leads to mistakes.

Creating ownership, getting an active "buy-in" for a program of change, even when it is largely supported in principle by teachers, requires hard work and a clear plan on the part of the school leader. Jackie, principal of Empresa Elementary School in Vista, California, talked about this process at her school when she began implementing RCCP.

> You need to involve all staff in the decision to implement a program like RCCP. Throughout the process we sent groups of staff members to each training cycle until every person who works at Empresa had received the [training]. The structure of the training encouraged staff to bond with one another and also to bond with the concepts taught.
>
> My part in the development process was to keep enthusiasm for the program alive and allow it to flourish. A leadership team of staff members and I met monthly to review how the program was being embraced and what strategies were needed to maintain our dream. We developed a multifaceted approach.
>
> A group of third-, fourth-, and fifth-graders were chosen to become Junior Ambassadors. Our well-trained problem-solvers visited all classrooms and presented RCCP lessons to other children. We recognized two children from each classroom monthly with a "Peacemakers Award." Classmates nominated and voted on who should receive these awards. Their pictures went up on the peacemakers board, and a free pizza luncheon was given to the award recipients. Recently we received a safety grant from the state of California and provided a 3-day advanced

peacemaking skills training for [the] fourth- and fifth-graders who became mediators at our school.

It was also important to maintain teacher enthusiasm for the program. In order to encourage staff to teach the RCCP lessons in the classroom, our RCCP mentor teacher, with the input from staff, identified 10 lessons for each grade level to teach. Then particular literature selections were identified and a lesson plan developed to support and extend learning for each of the RCCP lessons. Also, posters that highlight specific problem-solving strategies are prominently displayed in every classroom for consistency across grade levels.

Finally, it was extremely important that every person on this campus "talked the talk" as a model for students. When Vicki, the assistant principal, and I meet with children, staff, or parents we consistently model acceptance and problem-solving behavior. Our hope is that when children are faced with a problem they will be able to successfully have their needs met without hurt feelings or anger becoming physical. On occasion, we have also mediated staff conflict. Since they all talk the same talk, dealing with conflict has become, instead of a confrontation, a strategy session on how to accomplish a goal better. We problem solve anger into understanding.

Jackie's explanation gives some important insights into how this work begins to become a natural part of the school. Teachers participate in finding new and creative ways to teach the lessons, conduct schoolwide activities, and create their own variations of the work—variations that are strong, sustainable components of the program and clearly reflective of their particular school's culture. When this kind of ownership and involvement happens, those leading the innovation can step back just a little, while never relinquishing their support or ceasing to model the skills themselves in all they do.

Patience is an important part of the process too—knowing that not everybody's going to come along right away and that some may always be resistant to any change. Even when you feel that you're well along, there will be hills and valleys. It's not uncommon for school members to want to see change happen immediately. This is just one of the many challenges administrators face in the process of integrating SEL into their schools. But the results make it worthwhile.

FACING THE FUTURE, MEETING THE CHALLENGES AS EDUCATIONAL LEADERS

In my work with superintendents, principals, teachers, and parents, I've asked hundreds of groups in the United States and other countries this question: "If you could go to bed tonight and wake up in the morning with the power to ensure that you could teach one thing to all the children of the world, what would it be?" The responses are similar no matter where I am or whom I ask: that children feel loved, that they know they have a purpose, that they learn tolerance and compassion, and that they have a sense of their interconnectedness with other people and with the natural world. As educators, how can we not consciously and systematically attend to that which we dearly feel matters most?

In a recent survey of 272 "global thinkers" from around the world, five shared values emerged: compassion, honesty, fairness, responsibility, and respect (Loges & Kidder, 1997). These values seem to be so universal that it appears they are agreed on regardless of one's religious or spiritual perspective. And when the American Association of School Administrators asked 50 education leaders a similar question—What would students need to know and be able to do to thrive during the next century?—civility and ethical behavior were on the list along with math and science (Uchida, 1996). So we seem to agree on some of the fundamental tasks of education and the fact that they extend beyond helping young people stay out of trouble and achieve academic competence. As we work toward operationalizing what it means to have caring schools of sound character, we will find ourselves needing to outline in greater detail the steps needed to strengthen the shared values such schools will embody.

The good news is that this work has begun. Already, we can read about many school systems across the country that have used the frameworks developed by social scientists to bring together under one umbrella various efforts for preventing "risky" or antisocial behavior among young people. This approach acknowledges that the development of social and emotional skills is a critical factor in school-based prevention efforts, and it calls for an integration of the cognitive and affective domains for all students as a means of enhancing their chances for academic and personal success.

How successful will educational administrators and leaders be in welcoming a comprehensive approach to SEL in our schools? It will depend on how honestly those of us who are struggling to live an integrated life are willing to talk about and share our struggle with our more skeptical colleagues. And there are a few challenges ahead for those who want to give this movement some continued momentum.

Redefinition

We first have to continue to redefine what it means to be an educated person. This is a worldwide challenge to widen the vision of education beyond mastering a body of knowledge as measured on standardized tests. Even teachers who use our well-established RCCP are telling us that they are hanging on by a thread to make room for teaching our curriculum. It will help to meet the educational field where it is by acknowledging that academics are and always will be central. The new vision of education that we are talking about has the potential for producing students who not only have direction and purpose in life but who are also emotionally and socially skillful, and more academically competent as well. It is not an either-or situation, and we have to communicate that.

Rededication

The second challenge is for adults to let young people show us how we can help them cultivate their emotional, social, and inner lives, including openness and creativity. J. Robert Oppenheimer, one of the pioneers of nuclear energy, once said, "There are children playing in the streets who could solve some of the top problems in physics because they have modes of sensory perception that I lost long ago" (as cited in McLuhan & Fiore, 1984). Exploration, innovation, and creativity often come more easily to children and young people, and children are interested in life's most basic questions. Our task is to remember how integrated young children are and to find ways to protect that from being trampled on. This is part of teaching the whole child.

Sadly, as children move through our schools, they often receive spoken and unspoken messages that experiences related to their heart and spirit are not honored as part of their reality. The older they become, the more repressed, forgotten, and locked within themselves awareness and experience become. Adolescence offers an opportunity to reopen this line of inquiry, yet young people at this stage are usually met once again with the adult tendency to ignore or trivialize their experiences. What complicates matters is that few of us have experienced as learners the kind of holistic education we want to put into practice as teachers and administrators. If we hope to be part of bringing this work into schools, we will each need to find positive models and experiences that can show us how to live and teach in a more integrated way.

Research

The third challenge is to root this work in scientific research, as well as in sound pedagogy and child development theory. Current research in social and emotional learning and positive youth development has already begun to make the connection to school success; it is important that we encourage further work in this direction.

Reflection

Finally, we can't think about doing this work in classrooms without supporting teachers in the nurturing of their own emotional, social, and inner lives. Many of us want to help young people find a deeper sense of community and purpose, but we can't give what we don't have. In *The Courage to Teach* (1998), Parker Palmer wrote, "We teach who we are."

This work isn't about giving our students a road map. Effective teaching that has a lasting and deep impact on students must flow from the quality of each teacher's own inner life. One cannot know the subject area of one's teaching, and how to connect it meaningfully to the lives of students, without a strong sense of self-awareness and self-understanding (Palmer, 1998). And the best teaching is matched to the soul of one's students, a process that cannot be successful if a teacher is distant from his or her own soul.

Nel Noddings, educator and author of *The Challenge to Care in Schools* (1992), beautifully summed up the kind of education that blends emotional intelligence and intellectual development.

> I have argued that education should be organized around themes of care rather than traditional disciplines. All students should emerge in a general education that guides them in caring for self, intimate others, global others, plants, animals, and the environment, the human-made world and ideas. Such an aim doesn't work against intellectual development or academic achievement. On the contrary, it supplies a firm foundation for both. (Noddings, 1992)

And Daniel Goleman wrote,

> This new focus moves some of the key elements of emotional intelligence into a deeper dimension. Self-awareness takes on a new depth of inner exploration; managing emotions becomes self-discipline; empathy becomes a basis for altruism, caring, and compassion. And all of these basic skills for life can now be seen as building blocks of character. (Goleman, 2001)

A window of opportunity exists right now in the field of education for heart and spirit to enter. We must use this opening to broaden this work even further, and we need to support each other and engage people of all persuasions in this unfolding process.

Our mission is to insist that we develop policies and approaches that enable all our children to have their human spirits uplifted and their emotional, social, and inner lives nourished as a normal, natural part of their schooling. It will take enormous courage and energy to work across existing boundaries. Far from being marginal or irrelevant, attention to these matters will help us achieve the equilibrium we need in this chaotic world; we must foster the compassion, insight, and commitment to community that will be necessary to tackle the deep emotional, social, political, and spiritual dilemmas of our time.

As I look at the huge problems our young people will inherit—racism, poverty, violence, terrorism, the degradation of nature—I can't imagine how we will make it if we leave heart and spirit out. Educational leaders must be at the forefront of finding ways to ensure that no child is left behind and that the human mind, heart, and spirit all are welcomed in our homes, communities, and especially our schools.

REFERENCES

Goleman, D. (2001). Foreword. In L. Lantieri (Ed.), *Schools with spirit: Nurturing the inner lives of children and teachers* (pp. ix–x). Boston: Beacon.

Loges, W. E., & Kidder, R. M. (1997). *Global values, moral boundaries: A pilot survey.* Comden, ME: Institute for Global Ethics.

McLuhan, M., & Fiore, Q. (1984). *The medium is the message.* New York: Bantam.

Noddings, N. (1992). *The challenge to care in schools: An alternative approach to education.* New York: Teachers College Press.

Palmer, P. J. (1998). *The courage to teach: Exploring the inner landscape of a teacher's life.* San Francisco: Jossey-Bass.

Patti, J. (1996). *Perceptions of the peer mediation component of a school-wide conflict resolution program: Resolving conflict creatively.* Unpublished Ed.D. dissertation, Northern Arizona University.

Uchida, D., with Cetron, M. & McKenzie, F. (1996). *Preparing students for the twenty-first century.* Arlington, VA: American Association of School Administrators.

CHAPTER FOURTEEN

Institutionalizing Programming for Social–Emotional Learning

Lessons and Illustrations From the Field

Linda Bruene Butler

Jeffrey S. Kress

Jacqueline A. Norris

THE CHALLENGE OF SCHOOLWIDE IMPLEMENTATION

Recent incidents of school violence, along with a growing understanding of the implications of allowing bullying and other forms of peer harassment to go unchecked, have prompted school officials around the country to look for solutions to these problems. They want to know what can be done to get children to become more caring, responsible, and respectful of themselves and others. In short, they want to know how to make their children more socially and emotionally literate.

Daniel Goleman's book *Emotional Intelligence* (1995) has helped to promote worldwide awareness of the importance of social and emotional learning (SEL) and an interest on the part of school personnel to implement SEL programming. Guidelines for such programming were established in 1997 with the publishing of *Promoting Social and Emotional Learning: Guidelines for Educators* (Elias et al., 1997). This monograph provides teachers and administrators with a framework for organizing methods for teaching SEL skills. Educators are well aware that implementing a program in a school is no guarantee that it will become a lasting part of the school culture. Many program implementers are beginning to look ahead and ask, "How do we keep SEL programs from joining the ranks of the dusty curricula sitting unused on the top shelf and move toward making SEL programming a part of the everyday routine in our schools?" This is the daunting question that we discuss in this chapter.

The process of bringing an innovation or new practice into a school can be thought of as occurring in three stages: (1) the decision to adopt a program, (2) training for program implementation, and (3) institutionalization of programming (Commins & Elias, 1991). Institutionalization refers to permanent organizational change. When educational practices are institutionalized, observable and significant changes occur in "the way we do things around here," and these changes are sustained after training and initial implementation occurs. SEL programs that have been introduced in school districts to date often have not achieved systematic and coordinated institutionalization (Gottfredson, Wilson, & Najaka, 2001). An appreciation of the difficulties in reaching this end can help us understand why this is the case. Simply gaining consensus within a building or district regarding the best model and methods is a process that can take months or years. Once that is achieved, gaining the resources and materials needed for staff training is also a complex endeavor. And all of this must happen before any teacher training takes place. Once training occurs, the adult learners must implement the program with fidelity if positive outcomes are to occur, but initiating and maintaining the effort it takes to integrate new skills if often difficult.

Our basic premise for working toward institutionalization is that this outcome must be kept in clear focus throughout the program planning, training, and consultation processes. Certain supports can be put in place that can help make institutionalization more likely (Heller & Firestone, 1996; Hord, Rutherford, Huling-Austin, & Hall, 1987; Kress, Cimring, & Elias, 1997; Norris, 1998; Sarason, 1996). Although there is no magic recipe for this, in the course of our work with the Social Decision Making/Problem Solving model (for more information about this program, see Elias & Bruene Butler, 1999; Elias & Clabby, 1992; Elias & Tobias, 1996), we have learned, along with our school-based collaborators, many innovative ideas for setting up supports for institutionalization. Our goal is to share some of these ideas. We frame these recommendations with case examples from pioneering districts.

SUPPORTS FOR INSTITUTIONALIZATION

Link SEL Programming With Primary and Priority Functions of the Organization

Guidelines for educators to promote SEL published by the Association for Supervision and Curriculum Development (Elias et al., 1997) state that students benefit most from a combination of curriculum-based instruction and ongoing, infused opportunities to practice skills from preschool to high school. If SEL is seen as an "add-on" or something that is up to the individual teacher to provide when there is "time," effective implementation is unlikely to occur. Teachers report feeling that the demands of their current curriculum are already overwhelming. In successful SEL sites, administrators take an active role in the detailed problem solving and planning to design a realistic strategy for when and how SEL instruction and practice will occur. A variety of approaches have been used in some of our most successful schools to ensure a strong and permanent foothold within the core operations of the school. Some examples include the following:

Infusing SEL Skills Into the Board-Approved Curriculum

Curricula are the building blocks that schools use to set forth an organizational plan for teaching objectives across the grade levels, and because of this, they can be used as the vehicle for integrating social and affective development and learning into formal and regulated school operations. When an SEL curriculum and instructional plan becomes part of the curriculum approved by the school board, the importance of, and accountability for, teaching such skills is highlighted. The development of a plan with administrative and school board support has been a key strategy for establishing stable and effective programming. The specifics of the plan, however, have varied within each setting. For example, in Clifton, Cape May Special Services School District, Highland Park, and in many other New Jersey school districts, a scope and sequence of skills for the elementary grades, developed with teacher input, has become an approved part of the curriculum taught by the classroom teachers. In St. Charles, Illinois, a districtwide plan for SEL programming was adopted as a foundation for substance abuse prevention, conflict resolution, and character education. St. Thomas Moore Cathedral School in Arlington, Virginia, has developed a scope and sequence of skills that are taught and practiced within their religious education curriculum. Teachers then develop specific plans for extending the practice and application of these same skills within the academic curriculum and within school policies for addressing real-life problems and decisions. In North Caldwell, New Jersey, educators were trained in skills of curriculum mapping using the Social Decision Making/Problem Solving curriculum as the model for teaching and practicing the process. The finished products also helped other teachers to see how the SEL program was an integral component of other academic curriculum.

Linking With National and State Standards, Standardized Testing, and Grades

In our most successful SEL school sites, consistent efforts to align SEL teaching and objectives with state and national standards and testing are essential in helping teachers implement SEL instruction with fidelity. Despite the fact that many individual teachers recognize the value of SEL, many educators today feel primarily accountable for standardized test scores. In fact, for many teachers and principals, they are criteria for reappointment. Test scores are usually published in local newspapers and are often seen by parents and communities as a benchmark of educational attainment—and thus of their educators' professional competence. Norris and Kress (2000) described a process and outcomes of activities that map the overlap between social and emotional learning skills and the New Jersey Core Curriculum Standards. These illustrations of the strong overlap of SEL with the state standards has been used to help teachers realize that by focusing on SEL they are doing exactly what they should be doing.

In Highland Park, North Caldwell, and Westwood (NJ), benchmarks for grade levels linked with core curriculum standards have been adopted. In Highland Park and South Plainfield (NJ), SEL skills have been included on the report card. Linking SEL with testing and grades is one of the most effective ways to ensure that institutionalization will occur.

Linking SEL to Existing Mandates for Annual Goal Setting or Themes

SEL objectives have also been targeted as a school or district goal for which there is accountability for achieving measurable outcomes. Piscataway (NJ) selected goals in the area of social competence to be a part of their pupil performance objectives, which is part of their state's annual quality assurance report. Developing a series of strategic objectives over a multiyear period has been particularly helpful for building stable and comprehensive SEL programming in numerous school districts. Targeting SEL training and implementation goals within a teacher's Professional Improvement Plan (PIP) and in a student's Individual Educational Plan (IEP) also serve to position SEL in line with priority and mandated operations. Less formally, some schools and districts adopt annual SEL-related themes, such as Respect or Honesty (Pasi, 2001), and these promote obvious inroads for SEL instruction and content.

Establishing New Roles for SEL Leadership and Management

One common difficulty faced in the process of developing integrated and comprehensive SEL programming in schools is that existing job roles are already full and demanding. Therefore, it is often difficult for anyone to add on leadership and management tasks regarding logistics, planning, and ongoing monitoring of SEL program activities. The development of SEL Committees, or Leadership and Management Teams, has been helpful in providing the ongoing support that is needed for establishing and integrating SEL programming and the continuous quality improvement efforts needed to keep this programming viable and effective.

SEL committees work to develop program objectives, action plans, and budgets each year. SEL objectives generally include issues of training and technical support for teachers who are new or teaching different grade levels from past years; conducting activities for parent awareness, involvement, and training; evaluating program effectiveness; and planning for adaptations, expansion, and improvements needed to respond to new demands or student and community needs.

The composition of the SEL committee will vary, but most often representatives include administration; child study team members; school counselors; teacher representatives from different grades, special education, "specials"; and, whenever possible, playground or cafeteria aides and parents. In several districts such as Cape May Special Services and Berkeley Heights school districts in New Jersey, the entire team of educators involved in the initial pilot program met every month to assess progress and to problem solve implementation issues. As the program grew and expanded, the committee structure changed to include representatives from different buildings who attend district committee meetings. The team, consisting of a representative within each building, serves as a support and resource, responsible for monitoring the program, providing support to new teachers, discussing program progress and problems at staff and grade level meetings, and coordinating activities for parents and students with special needs.

In addition to the committee, establishing an SEL coordinator, or chairperson, with specified responsibilities can help ensure that tasks such as arranging meetings, distributing and collecting documents and evaluation measures, liaising with building representatives and program consultants, and other middle-management functions are not left to chance. This often results in a formal job role modification in which, depending on the scope of the task within an individual site, a specified amount of time, such as a half a day per week, 3 days per week, or full time have been allocated within or as the individual job description.

Attending to the Needs of Adult Learners

The field of SEL is at a unique point in its history. The majority of teachers today have neither received training in SEL programming in their preservice training nor were they formally taught these skills when they were in elementary and middle school. However, many have been addressing SEL within their educational practices for many years as part of their individual approach to teaching. Traditional instructional methodology—thinking in terms of a scope and sequence of skills, using a systematic approach across grade levels—is a "new idea" in SEL.

As such, the learning curve of program implementers is quite varied. Some educators have already been doing effective, "SEL-friendly" activities but are now being asked to make their teaching more systematic and coordinated with instruction at adjacent grade levels. On the other hand, some teachers may be using techniques that are contradictory to SEL ideas (for example, providing negative feedback to students, using sarcasm, or not modeling effective self-calming) and now must face the prospect of their own major behavioral change. We must also bear in mind that any new instructional methodology must be worked into the context of an already full curriculum, across classrooms with compositions that may be quite varied in terms of behavioral needs and assets.

Because educators, as adult learners, have such diverse needs, many of our most successful schools have developed ways to provide ongoing follow-up, support, and technical assistance as teachers learn to implement SEL in an organized and systematic way. Initial staff development training is seen in these districts only as a launching point to program implementation that must be followed by continued opportunities for teachers to develop their own social and emotional abilities and their SEL teaching skills. This follow-up can take many forms, such as follow-up visits by an outside professional trainer or consultant or a within-district master teacher or certified trainer; discussions held as a regular part of staff or grade level meetings; opportunities to work with experienced teachers within or outside the district; and networking via Internet or distance learning technologies (Bruene Butler, Elias, Papke, Schweitzer, & Brown, in press).

In Highland Park (NJ), experienced teachers are provided with release time to mentor new teachers. In Jersey City (NJ), the budget for training was designed to provide teachers with technical assistance on site, after Saturday training sessions had occurred. Teacher feedback and consultant's anecdotal recordings of what occurred during onsite visits from program consultants documented that follow-up support was often critical and served as an initiating prompt for implementation to occur. For example, a young male teacher provided excellent ratings for the staff development workshop and stated, "I have never been as excited to try the new ideas covered in this workshop when I get back to my class." Despite this enthusiasm and perceived motivation, records from follow-up consultation visits indicated that 4 weeks of scheduled follow-up visits occurred; however, no lesson implementation took place. Instead, a fight involving a desk being thrown across the room, a mandated school assembly related to whole-school reform, and testing demands became the priority. Teacher surveys, distributed after the first year of implementation, indicated that the newly trained teachers found the onsite follow-up to be one of the most helpful aspects of the program, and for many, these were the prompts and support needed to persist in their efforts to implement a new program and find ways to overcome the obstacles within their classrooms (Wattenmaker, Elias, & Bruene Butler, 2001).

Efforts to Go Beyond the "Wish And Hope" Method of Developing Classroom Applications

We have found that structured curricula and lesson plans can be helpful to a teacher in the beginning stages of learning to provide direct instruction of SEL abilities. Once teachers learn to teach the skill, however, the next step is to combine this instruction with ongoing opportunities to practice skills both within academic content and in real life. In our experience, the ability to weave SEL concepts into critical points in a story, a current events lesson, a historical discussion, or a real-life complex emotional problem or conflict is a skill that requires repeated guided practice and support. Ongoing structured opportunities for supportive practice helps teachers as learners to internalize new methods and processes and allows them to become increasingly skillful at recognizing and developing SEL applications.

St. Charles, Illinois, was one of our first districts to identify a team of teachers who were particularly skilled at creating application activities and identifying ways to infuse skill practice within their other academic curricula. The district paid these teachers for summer curriculum development so that they could document the lesson plans they had used, as well as create additional application activities. These "field-tested" products were then distributed to other teachers as useable examples of curriculum application.

In Piscataway, an *SEL Exchange* newsletter was compiled five times a year. This document included a district-level progress report; detailed lesson ideas developed by teachers at the primary, intermediate, and middle school levels for infusing the practice of SEL skills into content areas; and a question-and-answer and input section for teachers to engage in collaborative problem solving, discussion of current issues, and sharing of tips. Recently, the *Exchange* has evolved into a within-district e-mail-based bulletin board. One of the features on our training office Web site (www.umdnj.edu/spsweb) is the Roving Reporter. Innovative lesson plans, student accommodations, ideas for involving parents, staff development activities, and other aspects of program implementation are compiled to share with other school sites.

Planned Extensions of SEL Within and Beyond the School Walls

Classroom-based instruction and practice of SEL is an important first step in addressing SEL skills; however, some of our most exciting work has happened when children and teachers have extended their skill-building efforts to different settings within the school, as well as beyond the school walls. This process not only reinforces SEL skills for students but also helps embed SEL efforts more deeply within the contexts of the school and community, thereby strengthening efforts at institutionalization.

SEL skills learned in the classroom can be *practiced throughout the school.* The lunchroom, playground, and special subject areas (gym, art, and music) are all venues for SEL skill use. Educators in

Highland Park have integrated SEL skills within the context of class- and buildingwide discipline and behavior management procedures. A Social Decision Making/Social Problem Solving Computer Lab (Poedubicky, Brown, Hoover, & Elias, 2001) has been designed to provide students with structured opportunities to think through a problem they are facing or that has occurred as a result of breaking a school rule. The Cape May Special Services School District, in Cape May Courthouse (NJ), has adapted their Outdoor Experiential Education Curriculum to provide infused opportunities to practice the specific SEL skills targeted by the classroom teachers at various grade levels.

Community service projects provide another powerful mode of SEL practice and extension. In 1999, sixth-grade students in both public and private schools in Piscataway came together to address the goal of reducing vandalism in the community. Using the SEL skills learned in their classes (such as problem solving, goal setting, setting criteria, and effective communication), students use e-mail, the Internet, and faxes to share ideas, ask questions, and get feedback on this issue from their peers, as well as the mayor, the police chief, and the director of recreation. Representatives from each class met at a convocation held in the spring to share their school's suggested solution to the problem. Using a technology laboratory in each building, the students not in attendance were able to provide input to the event via video conferencing. The representatives, after coming to consensus among all the schools, then presented what they believed to be the most effective plan and evaluation strategy to city officials for review by the town council (Dencker, 1999). This meaningful practice of SEL skills and technology also provided students with an experiential opportunity to learn about the operations of the municipality, thus addressing an area of the core curriculum and the school district's mission to build civic awareness and concern among its youth. The town council approved the creation of three billboards within the town to display antivandalism messages developed by the students. The students worked as discussion group leaders to make elementary-aged students aware of the economic and emotional cost of vandalism to their community. Screensavers were created for the high school computer labs so that the messages would be an ever-present part of the students' environment. As seventh- and eighth-graders, those original students have continued to monitor and evaluate the effectiveness of their plans.

In Berkeley Heights (NJ), fifth- and sixth-graders participate in projects to improve the environment. Through the years, their efforts have resulted in presentations to the New Jersey State Assembly, petitions to local government that resulted in plastics recycling in the community, starting and monitoring a recycling program in the school cafeteria, and conducting a fundraising project to plant trees in the community to avoid soil erosion, to name a few of the projects they have undertaken.

Involving parents is an important facet of entrenching SEL efforts, but one that requires creative and innovative strategies to achieve. In several school districts, such as Berkeley Heights, Old Bridge, Clifton, and Piscataway (NJ), to name a few, local cable television stations have been used to air programs that inform parents about SEL activities at school, and to provide concrete ideas for parents to promote these skills at home. These programs can be shown at a variety of times identified through a parent survey as most convenient for viewing. In addition, videotape copies can be borrowed from the school or viewed at the school for those families without means to view at home. Teachers in St. Charles, Illinois, and in Glen Ridge, New Jersey, have designed homework assignments and parent involvement activities. In Highland Park, NJ, parent awareness information is provided on the school Web site.

Training Other Adults in the Community to Reinforce and Practice SEL Skills

When other adults in students' lives learn the SEL methods and language used by school staff, it helps strengthen the connections of SEL programming to real-life applications. Staff from New Brunswick (NJ) Youth Services system are trained in the SEL methods used in the classroom and in how to promote the use of these skills in after-school and summer programs. In Somerville (NJ), community sports coaches are trained to use SEL prompts, such as "Keep Calm" and "Listening Position" within the context of sports events and goal setting.

Sharing Innovations and Effective Practices

Once educators have been trained in effective SEL methods, they can become the true experts and masters of making this work effective and meaningful to their students. Providing educators using SEL methods, whether within a school or from a variety of sites in the district, with opportunities to share effective practices with each other through local conferences or visits are powerful professional development experiences. Currently, we are in the process of establishing a Network of Schools for SEL using distance learning technology. The use of video conferencing allows for co-teaching or observing an experienced educator; administrators receiving assistance from out-of-district leadership teams; students working with peers from other schools on SEL activities; and increased contact with SEL consultants. Online training modules can be a powerful fortification and extension of live training sessions by providing educators with a variety of sample lessons and activities that they can adopt and opportunities to observe a variety of master teachers in action. Such a support network can serve to keep SEL efforts up to date and provide teachers with SEL role models and boosters.

CONCLUSION

We are at an exciting time in terms of SEL programming. More and more, educators are realizing that students' acquisition of these skills is too important to leave to chance. We have worked in many pioneering districts where SEL efforts are making the same point about teachers' SEL programming efforts. Institutionalization of SEL requires effort and planning. Good intentions are a wonderful start, but they are not enough. Systems can and must be put in place to ensure the longevity of SEL programming. We hope that the examples we have presented from an array of districts in which we have worked will energize others. We encourage the reader to use these examples as springboards for creative planning, and to adapt and expand these examples as we all learn to become more effective in this critical area of student learning.

REFERENCES

Bruene Butler, L., Elias, M., Papke, M., Schweitzer, H., & Brown, R. (In press). Developing a network of schools for social and emotional learning. In R. Stern & T. Repa (Eds.), *Social emotional learning and new digital means.* Social and Emotional Learning Series. New York: Teachers College Press.

Commins, W. W., & Elias, M. J. (1991). Institutionalization of mental health programs in organizational contexts: The case of elementary schools. *Journal of Community Psychology, 19,* 207–220.

Dencker, M. (1999, May 27). Vandalism as learning tool. *Star Ledger* (Newark, NJ), p. 18.

Elias, M. J., & Bruene Butler, L. (1999). Social decision making and problem solving: Essential skills for interpersonal and academic success. In J. Cohen (Ed.), *Educating minds and hearts: Social emotional learning and the passage into adolescence* (Series on Social Emotional Learning). New York: Teachers College Press.

Elias, M. J., & Clabby, J. F. (1992). *Building social problem solving skills: Guidelines from a school-based program.* San Francisco: Jossey-Bass.

Elias, M. J., & Tobias, S. E. (1996). *Social problem solving interventions in the schools.* New York: Guilford. (Available from www.nprinc.com)

Elias, M. J., Zins, J. E., Weissberg, R. P., Frey, K. S., Greenberg, M. T., Haynes, N. M., Kessler, R., Schwab-Stone, M. E., & Shriver, T. P. (1997). *Promoting social and emotional learning: Guidelines for educators.* Alexandria, VA: Association for Supervision and Curriculum Development.

Goleman, D. (1995). *Emotional intelligence.* New York: Bantam.

Gottfredson, D. C., Wilson, D. B., & Najakda, S. S. (2001). School-based crime prevention. In D. P. Farrington, L. W. Sherman, & B. Welson, B. (Eds.), *Evidence-based crime prevention.* London: Routledge.

Heller, M. F., & Firestone, W. A. (1995). Who's in charge here? Sources of leadership for change in eight schools. *Elementary School Journal, 96,* 65–66.

Hord, S. M., Rutherford, W. L., Huling-Austin, L., & Hall, G. E. (1987). *Taking charge of change.* Alexandria, VA: Association for Supervision and Curriculum Development.

Kress, J. S., Cimring, B. R., & Elias, M. J. (1997). Community psychology consultation and the transition to institutional ownership and operation of intervention. *Journal of Educational and Psychological Consultation, 8,* 231–253.

Norris, J. A. (1998). *Promoting social competence and reducing violence and negative social interactions in a multicultural school setting.* Unpublished doctoral dissertation, Graduate School of Education, Rutgers University, New Brunswick, NJ.

Norris, J. A., & Kress, J. S. (2000, May–July). Reframing the standards vs. social and emotional learning debate: A case study. *The Fourth R, 91.*

Pasi, R. (2001). *Higher expectations: Promoting social emotional learning and academic achievement in your school* (Social and emotional learning series) New York: Teachers College Press.

Poedubicky, V., Brown, L., Hoover, H., & Elias, M. J. (2000–2001). Using technology to promote health/decision making. *Learning and Leading with Technology, 28*(4), 19–21, 56.

Sarason, S. B. (1996). *Revisiting "The culture of the school and the problem of change."* New York: Teachers College Press.

Wattenmaker, W., Elias, M. J., & Bruene Butler, L. (2001). *Jersey City Public Schools, Evaluation Report, and Social Decision Making/Problem Solving Program: Preliminary Report.* In-house document, New Jersey City Public Schools.

CHAPTER FIFTEEN

Implementing a Social–Emotional Learning Program

Stories From Schools

Carol Apacki

Implementing a comprehensive social and emotional learning program is a process, not an event. It requires a shared vision and coordinated strategy for addressing young people's healthy development. It involves a long-term commitment, support, and collaboration among schools, families, students, and community members. The result is a more vital school community to help students become capable and contributing members of society.

One of the best ways to understand the process is to follow the stories of schools that have successfully implemented a social–emotional learning (SEL) program. These are not extraordinary schools, other than in their commitment to the full education of their students' minds and hearts. What they have accomplished is attainable by the vast majority of schools with capable leadership. The learning from these schools, plus dozens of others that have been studied, is synthesized here to yield some general principles of implementation success across multiple school settings.

IMPLEMENTING IN ONE SCHOOL IN A DISTRICT: LEXINGTON ELEMENTARY, MONROE, LOUISIANA

When Lynn Hodge became principal of Lexington Elementary School 5 years ago, she and her staff knew they needed to do something different. Attendance rates and standardized test scores were down, and there were far too many suspensions and office referrals. She says, "We were ready to do something new, so when I heard about a training workshop for a new comprehensive life skills program, I invited our staff to attend."

Teachers and support staff went together. Reflecting on the experience 5 years later, she says the following:

> We got what we were looking for. The training brought us together before school started in the fall. We laughed, talked, and worked as a team. The program's comprehensive framework helped us create a shared vision of what we wanted to achieve with our students. The lessons presented the critical skills and provided a common experience and language for everyone in the school about more positive ways to deal with one another. In the process, we became more cohesive as a school community.

Today at Lexington Elementary, classroom time is set aside each week for teaching children the emotional and social skills related to five thematic topics, "Building a School Community," "Growing as a Group," "Making Positive Decisions, "Growing Up Healthy and Drug-Free," and "Celebrating You and Me." Teachers begin with a 20–30 minute core lesson, and then students practice using the specific skills in various subject areas, such as language arts, health, art, and social studies. Thematic topics are the same across the grade levels; however, the skills within each topic are sequential and developmentally appropriate. This thematic approach builds a shared understanding and sense of community throughout the school. Parents get actively involved, too. Through a parent–child activity booklet, they are able to reinforce at home the skills their children are learning at school.

To ensure that students apply the skills they are learning in real-life situations, each class takes responsibility for planning and carrying out a service-learning project. Students choose what they want to do. One year, for example, a class of fifth-grade students used their collaborative groupwork skills to collect supplies for victims of hurricane Mitch. They posted signs around the community and gathered food, bedding, and other staples. The local newspaper wrote an article about their efforts. Lynn believes that these projects strengthen students' connections to their community. She says, "Since so many of our young people stay in our area, they need to know they have a voice in making the community a good place to be."

Recently, Lexington Elementary had the highest nationally normed test scores in the district, as well as the highest student and teacher attendance. Lynn credits these results to a more supportive learning environment. Student attitudes and conduct have improved, and the number of suspensions and discipline referrals has decreased. She explains,

> We all can feel and see the difference. Our students are more responsible. I see them using their conflict management skills, and they can listen and work together. Using a comprehensive program like this has given us something we could all hold onto—and that has really made a difference in our school.

IMPLEMENTING IN MULTIPLE SCHOOLS IN A DISTRICT: ANOKA SCHOOL DISTRICT, ANOKA, MINNESOTA

It all started when the Oxbow Creek Elementary School Site Council adopted Lions-Quest Skills for Growing to address its need for a schoolwide character education initiative. Skills for Growing is one example of a comprehensive SEL program for Grades K–5. The program helps schools prepare children for the responsibilities of family life, citizenship, and future employment by teaching them the skills and behaviors that support self-discipline, responsibility, good judgment, and respect for self and others. Children learn these skills through classroom instruction and skill practice, peer interaction and discussion, and service-learning projects in the school and community. Program materials involve family and community members in all aspects of the program. Typically, 2- or 3-day staff development workshops are provided for each school's implementation team, along with follow-up support and additional staff development opportunities.

As word spread of the program's success, Oxbow Creek staff were invited to make presentations to staff in other schools. Local Lions Clubs offered to raise funds for training workshops for additional teachers. These workshops created such enthusiasm that, by the end of second year, 10 more schools had chosen to implement the program. By the fourth year, 22 of the 30 district schools had implemented Skills for Growing. Karen Dahl, a former Oxbow Creek teacher who now coordinates the program throughout the district, believes that " 'top-down' implementation of an SEL program does not work." Rather, buy-in needs to be cultivated at the individual school level.

Because so many elementary schools in Anoka are using Skills for Growing, the program has become an important vehicle for providing a framework, a coordinated strategy, and a shared language for districtwide prevention efforts. The program has also become visible in the community. Karen explains that

> We always start the school year by having someone dress up as the program mascot, Q-Bear, and go around and visit each school. He stands and greets people at the school doors. Everyone in the district knows and comes up to hug Q-Bear.

Local Lions Clubs have been integrally involved in Quest programs nationally and internationally by raising funds, attending trainings as community members, and helping in the schools. This also took place in Anoka. As the district coordinator, Karen says, "I feel supported by so many people—school administrators, school staff, parents, the Lions-Quest trainer, and local Lions Clubs members." The district maintains this support by sending new staff to workshop trainings and reenergizing existing staff with "Re-Quest" workshops. When Minnesota adopted new graduation standards, a program correlation guide was developed and distributed. Karen relates, "Now I can talk with an administrator or a parent more specifically about how the skills and concepts students are learning in Skills for Growing lessons fit with Minnesota's Comprehensive Goals."

Each school has its own site-based coordinator who oversees the program. To adapt and improve the program, these coordinators meet together to share ideas, resulting in more positive connections, team building, and collegiality across the district. Karen says,

> We want to continue our efforts in middle school with the Lions–Quest conflict management program, and in high school with youth service. When I think of what we have accomplished over the past four years, I have this image of all these hands making a circle. Inside the circle are all of our students.

IMPLEMENTING DISTRICTWIDE: CHULA VISTA ELEMENTARY SCHOOL DISTRICT, CHULA VISTA, CALIFORNIA

When the Chula Vista Elementary School District had to replace their old prevention curriculum, a district task force ordered several highly recommended programs. "We were looking for a program with a broad prevention focus that included all the elements and skills identified in the resiliency literature," explains Dale Parent, the district-level project coordinator. The task force developed criteria for program effectiveness and used it to grade the programs accordingly. Dale explains, "These criteria helped us select Lions-Quest Skills for Growing as the way to address what we in our school district already value."

Implementation began 5 years ago with a districtwide invitation to school staff to attend a Lions-Quest program workshop. The success of this first workshop led to several more that same year. Attending the workshop and using the program was never made mandatory. People got involved because they chose to do so. Dale says,

> Once teachers experienced the positive, supportive learning environment created at the workshop, they were eager to replicate such an atmosphere with students in their classrooms. They saw the Skills for Growing curriculum as a vehicle for helping them do this.

In that first year, 12 teachers volunteered and four were selected to become certified as "affiliate trainers"—or ATs—who train and provide ongoing support for all those in the district who are using the program. The four ATs received additional facilitation skill training from Quest program developers and copies of the workshop training materials. Four years later, as a result of their efforts, more than 400 teachers from 35 schools in Chula Vista are using Skills for Growing. To maintain and improve the program, the ATs take responsibility for running six workshops a year. Local Lions Clubs work as community partners in providing ongoing financial support.

The 3-day workshops, open to school staff members and parents from all the schools in the district, have become an important community-building effort in the district. People from various schools are getting to know one another, and participants are welcomed as honored guests. Lynn relates that teachers tell her, "You make us feel so special." A continental breakfast, a hot lunch, and coffee and sodas are served. She says that by "breaking bread" and having fun together, people in the district develop a sense of community among themselves. This is an important part of preparing teachers to implement the program and create a more supportive learning environment back in their own classrooms and schools.

Dale emphasizes the importance of involving others in the program besides teachers. She says, "Our school counselors, for example, use the program materials to build on key skills and concepts as they meet with children during the day." JuDee Smitko, a teacher and an AT, focuses on helping teachers actively engage parents through the Skills for Growing student-activity booklet and the parent meeting guide. Involving family members enables them to reinforce at home the skills their children are learning at school. She finds that the parent meetings lead to more parental involvement in the schools overall.

The ATs are critical to Chula Vista's success. They work hard to support teachers and make the program a vital part of school life. The message is, "If you're having problems, and you don't call me, then I am not doing my job." JuDee recognizes that the ATs try to make the program so easy and practical that teachers can say, "Ah, yes, I can do this!" Mentoring and supporting teachers helps them to feel empowered and enthusiastic about what they can accomplish together. JuDee explains, "Now that we know one another, people in the district are collaborating on new ways we can strengthen the program. So many good things are happening."

KEYS TO IMPLEMENTING A COMPREHENSIVE AND EFFECTIVE SEL PROGRAM

A comprehensive SEL program embraces a variety of aspects of a child's world. By providing a proactive and coordinated strategy for addressing children's social, emotional, physical, and ethical well-being, it serves an important "positive prevention" purpose. To be optimally effective, SEL initiatives should begin in kindergarten and continue in a developmentally appropriate sequence through high school. But realistically, one needs to begin where one can, with the goal of expanding developmentally. From the stories from schools just presented, as well as hundreds of other cases in the SEL literature and lore, key components and characteristics of an effective comprehensive program can be derived.

Key Components for SEL Implementation

A Classroom Curriculum

The curriculum has a positive prevention approach and a focus on a broad range of life skills. A curriculum forms the anchor, or foundation, of school or district SEL efforts. Lesson plans are developmentally appropriate and sequentially designed to reinforce the skill being presented across the grade levels. The age-appropriate learning experiences complement the school curriculum and provide ways to teach, integrate, and reinforce program concepts into the everyday life at school.

Positive School Climate

The SEL approach offers many different ways to build a caring and supportive learning environment through the curriculum activities and schoolwide projects, with multiple opportunities for collaboration among teachers, parents, students, and community members.

Professional Development and Ongoing Support

To ensure successful implementation of the program, all those overseeing or teaching the program should attend a program workshop to gain "hands-on" experiences with program materials and plan for effective implementation. Under the guidance of a skilled educator and facilitator, the workshop serves as a model of what should take place in the classroom. In addition, other program-related workshops and materials are available for ongoing support.

Family Involvement

Families play a vital role in shaping young people's learning experiences by serving on program planning teams, participating in parent–child SEL homework assignments, attending parenting workshops, and assisting with service-learning projects.

Community Involvement

Members of service organizations, businesses, law enforcement agencies, youth-serving organizations, and religious institutions are encouraged to participate through program workshops, school climate activities, panel discussions, service-learning projects, and school-sponsored parent meetings.

A General Time Frame for School or Districtwide Implementation

Effective implementation of an SEL program requires a long-term commitment of 3 or more years. It is a process that does not necessarily proceed in a linear, step-by-step fashion because schools may initiate the process differently, depending on the needs, levels of support, and resources available. Usually small groups of people begin and build momentum with the motto, "Start small—think big." In general, the SEL implementation time line follows these phases and involves the following activities:

Phase One: Planning for Implementation (Year 1)

- Determining needs
- Selecting a program that meets school goals
- Acquiring funds
- Building awareness with educators, parents, and community
- Developing a design for implementation and evaluation

Phase Two: Initiating Implementation (Years 1 and 2)

- Training staff, parents, and community members
- Putting program components into action
- Identifying technical assistance needs
- Providing follow-up support
- Developing a maintenance plan

Phase Three: Evaluating the Process and the Results (Years 2 and 3)

- Documenting the implementation process
- Determining the impact on staff, students, parents, and community

Phase Four: Adapting and Improving the Program (Years 3+)

- Improving, modifying, and enhancing
- Integrating into local goals and objectives

Phase Five: Institutionalizing the Program (Years 3+)

- Obtaining commitment and buy-in at all levels
- Acquiring long-term funding sources
- Initiating program replication, additional training, and ongoing support for additional classrooms and schools in the district

Administrative Tasks for Successful Initial Implementation of an SEL Program

Encouraging the adoption of a comprehensive SEL program like Lions-Quest Skills for Growing or any similar empirically supported SEL program identified by CASEL's program review, which is listed on their Web site (www.CASEL.org; see Chapter 2), can be initiated and facilitated by anyone in the school community, such as an administrator, school counselor, parent, or teacher. For SEL to be widely accepted, however, strong administrative support for implementation is important, as is guidance to ensure that implementation is a shared responsibility of building and district staff, parents, students, and community members.

How one gets started often lays the groundwork for future success in most school change contexts, and SEL is no different. Setting the stage for successful long-term implementation is related to the following administrative actions and considerations during the first two phases:

- *Programs address identified needs.* School staff, parents, and students can describe ways that the program meets identified needs of the school. For example, most schools use Lions-Quest programs to provide a comprehensive and skills-based approach to their prevention efforts, build sound character, promote active citizenship, and help establish safe, supportive environments for learning.
- *Collaborative decision making.* Selecting the program that will be the core of SEL skill building is a shared effort by school building staff. Family and community members are invited to participate in the planning process. As the process of training unfolds, training workshops incorporate staff development goals and the staff is given options about how the training and follow-up will be carried out.

- *Supportive, shared leadership.* The principal is an active advocate and is trained in the program. There is a broad base of support, with shared leadership among administration, teachers, and parents. Those involved have clear responsibilities and ownership for key program components: curriculum, school climate, service learning, and parent involvement.
- *Clear responsibilities and a commitment to role modeling.* Everyone involved in the program understands and feels committed to carrying out his or her program responsibilities. The school staff makes a conscious effort to model the positive behaviors taught in the lessons.
- *Fidelity with adaptation.* Schools make the program their own without leaving out the "quintessential" ingredients that are outlined in the program materials and training. District leadership ensures that neither a cookie-cutter nor a free-for-all approach is used.
- *Time factor addressed by administration.* The principal and teachers decide how and when they are going to teach the skill lessons. The administration provides time to do this.
- *Long-term commitment.* The administration and staff have made a long-term commitment to the program and plan together how they are going to implement program components. The implementation model is selected, and everyone understands how this fits into the everyday life of the school.
- *Active involvement of youth, parents, and community members.* Parents and community members know about the program, understand its purpose, and participate in the planning and implementation. Students share their ideas about schoolwide positive climate activities and possible service-learning projects.

Administrative Tasks to Facilitate Ongoing Success

From implementation histories in many schools, much has been learned about conditions that help keep SEL initiatives thriving, adaptive, and effective over long periods of time. Generally, the following need to be in place early, no later than Phase Three, if the skills of SEL are to become an integral part of school life:

- *Find an advocate at the district level.* Someone who has power and authority at the top and who supports the program and prevents its dilution or erosion.

- *Provide ongoing support for school staff.* There are program workshops for new staff and opportunities for staff to meet on a regular basis to discuss both successes and problems. The ATs are an example of ongoing support.
- *Select an on-site coordinator.* There is a "champion" who is funded by the district to oversee and coordinate program implementation, evaluation, and continuous improvement.
- *Accept financial responsibility at the district level.* The process for identifying and obtaining revenue to support the program is understood and regularized at the district level so that SEL is not solely dependent on unstable or unreliable sources of funding. The program is funded by hard as well as soft monies.
- *Arrange for ongoing evaluation.* Program evaluation is used to refine the program and make modifications and changes for the future and keep it responsive to changing needs, resources, and mandates.
- *Keep parents and community members involved.* Parents or community members are kept informed about the program. Concerns are addressed. They have many opportunities to actively participate in program activities.

SEL COMPETENCIES ADMINISTRATORS NEED TO FOSTER SCHOOLS OF SOUND EQ + IQ

The stories from schools about the conditions for implementing and maintaining SEL initiatives reflect the importance of vision setting, team building, collaborative decision making, and goal setting in the process. Doing these successfully requires that program stakeholders take responsibility for their own emotional intelligence. In fact, the extent to which emotional and social competencies are developed and modeled during program implementation will greatly influence a program's ultimate effectiveness. For administrators of schools that are successful in becoming places of sound character and strong SEL and emotional intelligence skills, linked to academic success, key competencies include the following:

- Recognizing and managing one's own emotions, strengths, and limits
- Initiating and managing change with openness to new opportunities, challenges, and information
- Building caring, collaborative relationships among school staff members, parents, and community members
- Communicating effectively, listening, and incorporating new ideas and perspectives
- Motivating, empowering, and working with others toward shared goals
- Using problem-solving skills to overcome obstacles and make needed adjustments
- Recognizing and affirming the abilities and contributions of others

Opportunities for program staff to develop and strengthen these competencies should be a critical part of professional development programs at all levels. This is best accomplished through interactive learning experiences, such as group discussions, presentations, and reflection on program philosophy and approach, which create shared understanding, language, and common purpose. There should be a variety of community-building experiences, along with "hands-on" practice in using program materials and strategies. As participants see and experience the power of emotional and social competencies in action, they begin to envision new ways of working together and with their students. This, in turn, fuels continuous growth of EQ and IQ for the benefit of students, school, and community.

Assessment Tools for Applying Social–Emotional Learning and Emotional Intelligence to Oneself and One's Students

ASSESSMENT TOOL 1: A RUDIMENTARY SELF-CHECK ON YOUR EMOTIONAL INTELLIGENCE

To further ground your understanding of social–emotional learning and emotional intelligence (SEL/EQ), consider this self-check on your own EQ in your administrative and leadership work:

1. How well do I know my own feelings?
   How well do I know the feelings of my staff?
   Board?

Students?
Think of a recent problem in the school. How were you feeling?
How were your children feeling?
How were others involved feeling?

2. How much empathy do I have for others, and how do I express it to them?
   When was the last time I expressed empathy?
   Am I sure others are aware of my concern for them?
   Am I able to understand another's point of view, even during an argument?

3. How do I cope with anger, anxiety, and other stresses?
   Am I able to maintain self-control when stressed?
   How do I behave after a hard day?
   How often do I yell at others?
   When are my best and worst times, and do these vary on different days?

4. What goals do I have for myself and my staff?
   What plans do I have for achieving those goals?

5. How do I deal with everyday, interpersonal problem situations?
   Do I really listen to others, especially by reflecting back to people what they are saying?
   Do I approach social conflicts in a thoughtful manner?
   Do I consider alternatives before deciding on a course of action?

ASSESSMENT TOOL 2: STANDARDS FOR DEVELOPING EMOTIONAL INTELLIGENCE IN THE CLASSROOM AND SCHOOL

Here is a beginning set of "standards" that can be applied to monitor and develop EQ in students. It takes the form of an "emotional intelligence report card" on which students of all grade levels can be rated, with attention to appropriate developmental levels as outlined in Elias et al. (1997). Use the following key to designate areas of strength and areas that need improvement:

+ = an area of current strength

? = an area in which there could be improvement, but it is not a top priority

− = an area in which improvement is a long-term goal

— = an area that is priority for current improvement and for which there is or will be an improvement plan

A. Self-Awareness

1. Recognize and name one's emotions

2. Understand the reasons for feeling as one does at various times

B. Management/Self-Regulation of Emotion

1. Verbalize and cope positively with anxiety, anger, depression

2. Improve impulse control, and reduce aggression, self-destructive, revengeful, antisocial behavior

3. Recognize strengths in and positive feelings about self, family, support network

C. Self-Monitoring and Performance

1. Focus clearly on tasks at hand

2. Set short- and long-term goals, modify performance in light of feedback

3. Mobilize positive motivation in self and others

4. Activate hope and optimism in self and others

5. Work toward optimal performance states, flow, and manage inverted U relationship between anxiety and performance in self and others

D. Empathy and Perspective Taking

1. Listen carefully and accurately

2. Increase empathy and sensitivity to others' feelings

3. Understand others' perspectives, points of view, feelings

4. Develop feedback mechanisms to improve the use of skills in everyday life

E. Social Skills in Handling Relationships

1. Manage emotions in relationships, harmonize

2. Express emotions effectively

3. Exercise assertiveness, leadership, persuasion, working as part of a team/cooperative learning group

4. Show consistent sensitivity to social cues

5. Display everyday social decision-making and problem-solving skills

6. Respond constructively and in a problem-solving manner to interpersonal and task obstacles

REFERENCE

Elias, M. J., Zins, J. E., Weissberg, R. P., Frey, K. S., Greenberg, M. T., Haynes, N. M., Kessler, R., Schwab-Stone, M. E., & Shriver, T. P. (1997). *Promoting social and emotional learning: Guidelines for educators*. Alexandria, VA: Association for Supervision and Curriculum Development.

Resources for Building Learning Communities Through Social–Emotional Learning and Emotional Intelligence

BOOKS AND MANUSCRIPTS

Ciarrochi, J., Forgas, J., & Mayer, J. (2001). *Emotional intelligence in every-day life*. Philadelphia: Taylor and Francis.

Cohen, J. (Ed.). (1999). *Educating minds and hearts: Social emotional learn-ing and the passage into adolescence*. New York: Teachers College Press.

Cohen, J. (Ed.). (2001). *Caring classrooms/intelligent schools: The social emotional education of young children*. New York: Teachers College Press.

Elias, M. J., Friedlander, B. S., & Tobias, S. E. (2001). *Engaging the resistant child through computers: A manual to facilitate social & emotional learning.* Port Chester, NY: National Professional Resources (*www.nprinc.com*; 1-800-453-7461).

Elias, M. J., & Tobias, S. E. (1996). *Social problem solving interventions in the schools.* Port Chester, NY: National Professional Resources/ Guilford Publishers (*www.nprinc.com*; 1-800-453-7461).

Elias, M. J., Tobias, S. E., & Friedlander, B. S. (2000). *Emotionally intelligent parenting: How to raise a self-disciplined, responsible, socially skilled child.* New York: Random House/Three Rivers Press.

Elias, M. J., Tobias, S. E., & Friedlander, B. S. (2002). *Raising emotionally intelligent teenagers: Guiding the way to compassionate, committed, courageous adults.* New York: Random House/Three Rivers Press.

Elias, M. J., Zins, J. E., Weissberg, R. P., Frey, K. S., Greenberg, M. T., Haynes, N. M., Kessler, R., Schwab-Stone, M. E., & Shriver, T. P. (1997). *Promoting social and emotional learning: Guidelines for educators.* Alexandria, VA: Association for Supervision and Curriculum Development.

Goleman, D. (1995). *Emotional intelligence: Why it can matter more than IQ.* New York: Bantam.

Lantieri, L. (Ed.). (2001). *Schools with spirit: Nurturing the inner lives of children and teachers.* Boston: Beacon.

Lantieri, L., & Patti, J. (1996). *Waging peace in our schools.* Boston: Beacon.

Norris, J. A., & Kress, J. S. (2000). Reframing the standards vs. social and emotional learning debate: A case study. *The Fourth R, 91,* 7–10.

Social and Emotional Learning. [Special issue]. (1997). *Educational Leadership, 54*(8).

Sylwester, R. (1995). *A celebration of neurons: An educator's guide to the human brain.* Alexandria, VA: Association for Supervision and Curriculum Development.

WEB RESOURCES

Collaborative for Academic, Social, and Emotional Learning: *www.casel.org.* (The CASEL Web site contains essays and other short articles on SEL and EQ and character education from many sources, including commentaries from *Education Week.*)

George Lucas Educational Foundation: *www.GLEF.org.*

Social Decision Making/Social Problem Solving Program: *www.umdnj. edu/spsweb.*

Character Education Partnership: *www.character.org.*

MEDIA

A variety of media resources and materials on SEL and EQ are available through *www.casel.org, www.nprinc.com, www.communitiesofhope.org,* and *www.6seconds.org.*

National Center for Innovation and Education. (1999). *Lessons for Life: How smart schools boost academic, social, and emotional intelligence.* Bloomington, IN: HOPE Foundation (*www.communitiesofhope. com;* a video inservice kit, especially for new teachers or teachers new to SEL/EQ).

Index